To order additional copies of this book, contact:
Xlibris LLC
0-800-056-3182
www.xlibrispublishing.co.uk
Orders@ Xlibrispublishing.co.uk

The Westbury Window
Unravelling a Victorian Entrepreneur

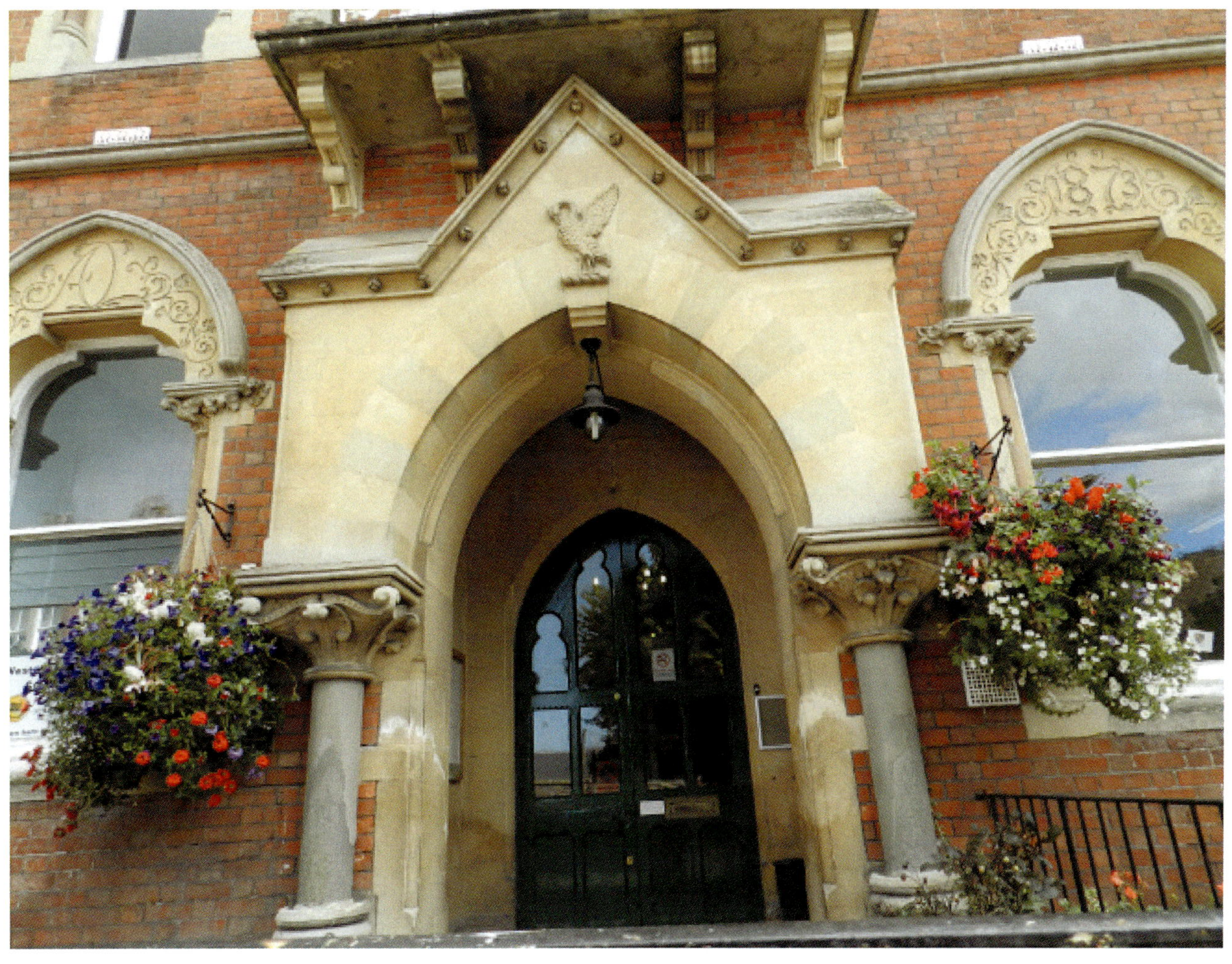

A portal in time and space
resonating to the voices of the Choir Invisible
and the salvation of William Shakespeare.

*Above is a photograph of the entrance to the Laverton Building,
Bratton Road, Westbury, Wiltshire today.*

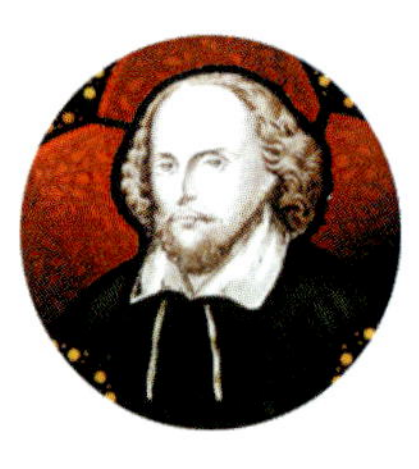

Shakespeare

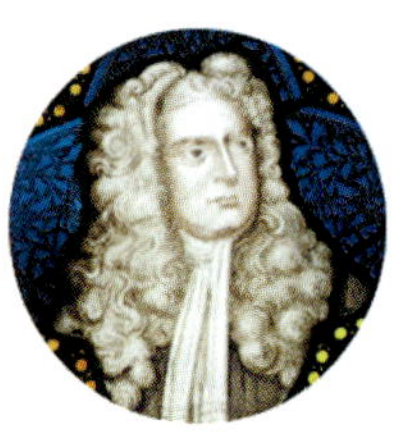

Newton

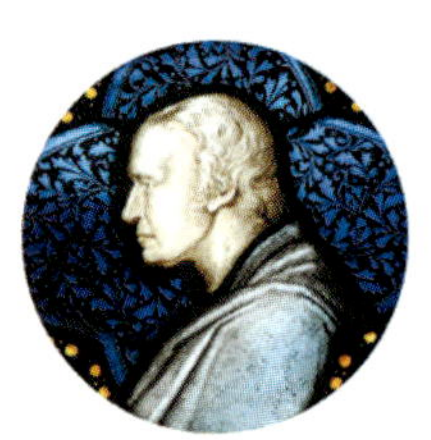

Watt

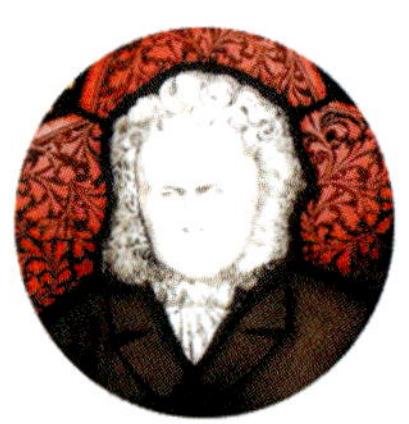

Landseer

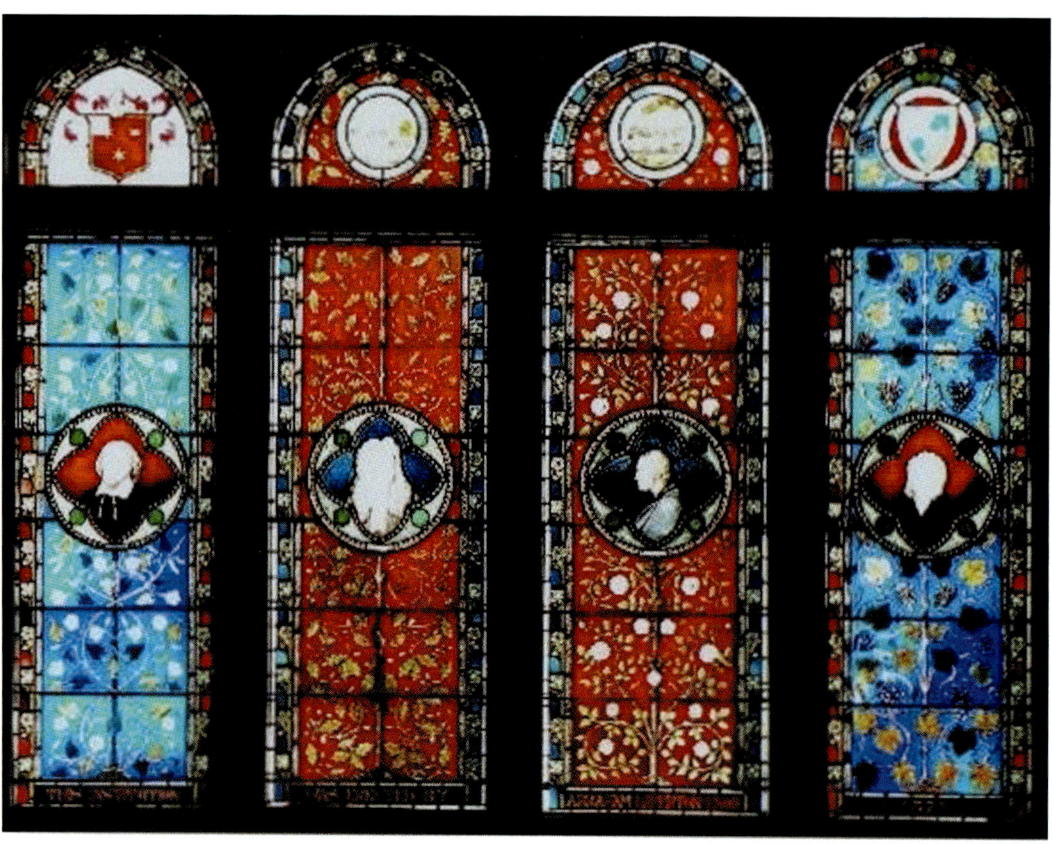

The four celebrated personages in the Westbury Window
and
the Westbury Window

This book is dedicated to all the people who work for Westbury Town Council.

'The finest of citizens, the best of places.'

The Laverton Pelican

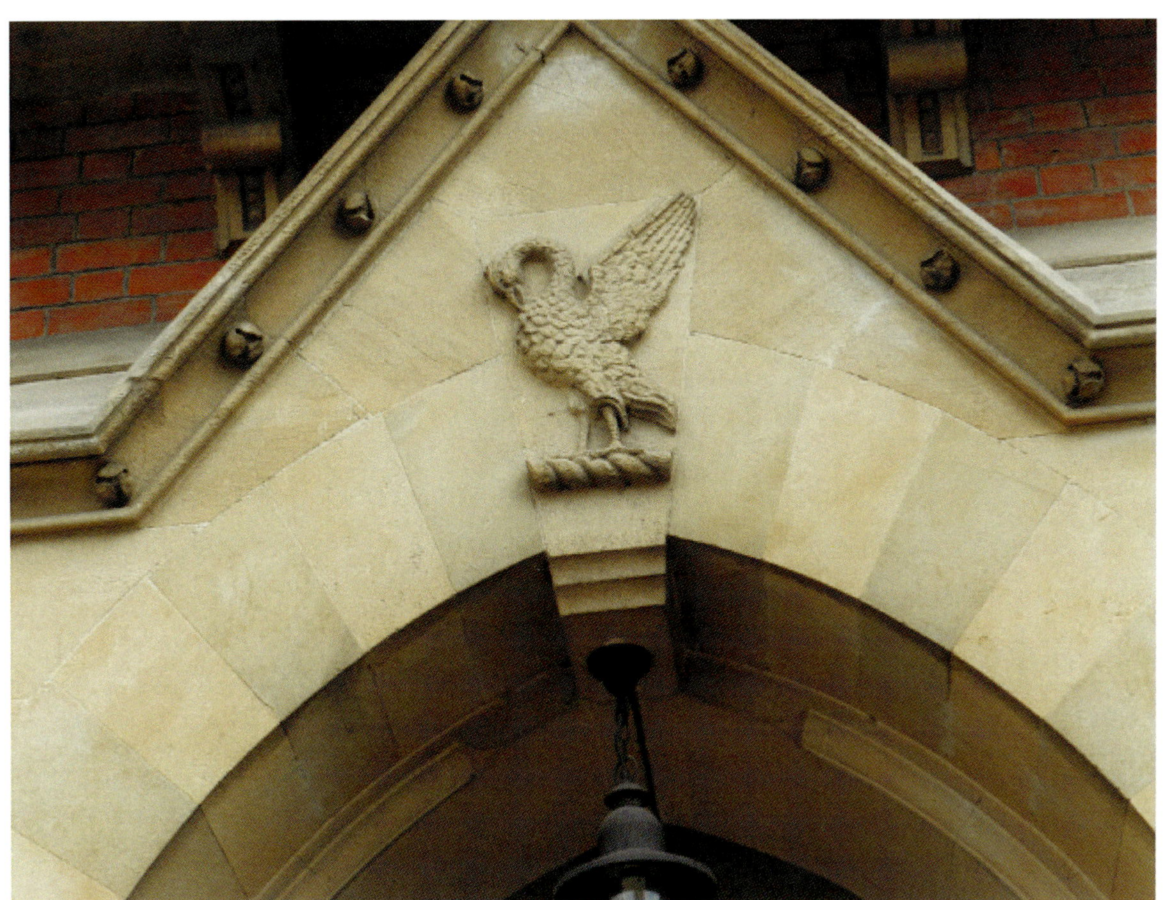

Frontispiece

John Powell has one aim in writing this book and that is to bring to the attention of the people of Westbury and the World the remarkable historical resource that is to be found in the town. To put it another way the people of Westbury need to take an intellectual ownership of this Window and have others come to admire its design, content and importance as an insight into the mentality of Victorian England and specifically one Victorian gentleman, Abraham Laverton.

In this first edition mistakes may be made, matters may be misinterpreted or missed altogether, key resources may emerge after the book has gone to print, psychic flak may spark and fly from those with grudges against the world and any imperfection set before them. Those things do not matter. For 140 years there is absolutely no record of anyone giving this Window more than a cursory glance and the genius who designed it lip service.

Getting this book into the public domain is the imperative for the Westbury Window is a most remarkable sectarian homily coded in ciphers and symbols, layered with scientific concepts and moralistic censure, conceived in more then four dimensions and executed so. It is an astronomical conundrum, an astrological timepiece, an alchemist's inspiration and an advocacy for restructuring time that sources its content from the ancient Chaldeans and Egyptians to the earliest Hebrew and Greek cultures and from Reformation Europe to the cosmological constant.

Those who have dismissed the Window for nearly six generations as a celebration of four great Britons must look again and ask themselves whether the extraordinary intellect of Abraham Laverton would have been satisfied with a legacy as bland as an advertising hoarding. To understand the Window is to begin to understand the man. It is complex, detailed, multifunctional, demanding to interpret, controversial and studded with ironic symbolism.

Those who are passers-by will see nothing in it. Those who pause and focus on the Window and beyond themselves will find the Universe at their feet.

About the Author

John Powell is a retired schoolteacher and has been living in Wiltshire for more than 12 years. He has written many articles for local newspapers, magazines, periodicals, and news letters on issues as varied as criticism of professional teaching associations, the Life of St. Fionntain of Ard Caoin (the story of an 8th century Irish prince in internal exile), the electronic espionage practiced by RAF Bomber Command during the Second World War and the importance of the adverb as a qualitative tool in assessing the socio-economic deprivation of pupils in UK schools at Key Stage 3.

For the last year he has been working on three books, the other two apart from this one being on travel that has been the great love of his life. This book has emerged as being the most compelling to finish because it contains revelations, insights, implications, accusations and controversies of importance. It presents new evidence about questions of national significance and not least it makes for a fascinating story about an extraordinary man.

That stated, travel even more than education has time and again been the determining factor influencing the life choices that have led him to where he is today. Together, travel and education provided the opportunity to have friendships with people such as former Labour government minister Dr Kim Howells and the splendid author and television figure Nicholas Crane whilst studying at what is now Anglia Ruskin University, Cambridge.

Travel and work placed him in the company of eccentric poet W H Auden who was encountered as a fascinating but controversial man as well as the Irish politician, historian, academic and writer Conor Cruise O'Brien who impressed as an extraordinary thinker and a man of powerful intellect and integrity.

Travel and his long term vocation in education provided the chance for encounters in his role as a part-time lecturer in local history and Irish studies (for various organizations including The Queen's University, Belfast and the Workers Education Association). Legendry academics such as Professor Ronnie Buchanan, Professor Noel Mitchel and Dr Fred Hammond attended classes he delivered whilst the former institution was one of four from where he also graduated.

Travel and friendships along with the above provided rare opportunities to play competitive sport (specifically rugby union) with a great friend, Irish international Ronnie Elliott and his all-time hero, the late Brian Thomas of Neath and Wales. Travel and adventure provided encounters with torture survivor Sheila Cassidy and planetary scientist Adriana Ocampo Uria that could never have been imagined. Without question the years spent travelling have provided John Powell with rich experiences that effectively opened the Window for him to look through it.

Foreword

Westbury, Wiltshire is a traditional West Country market town of around 11,000 citizens with a broader catchment area of some 45,000 people. The author of this book has been a resident of Westbury for more than 10 years. In that time he noticed two unusual features about buildings close to where he lives.

Firstly, in that time he has watched a spectacle of the refractions and reflections of the setting sun in midsummer upon the facades of the houses situated close to his own at a place named Prospect Square. On occasions it has been quite spectacular. These houses were built by one Abraham Laverton and their reflectivity is unusual but not unique.

Secondly, he has been curious about the alignment of the neighbouring and adjacent Laverton building that today houses the offices of Westbury Town Council. The building inspired curiosity because it appeared to have in one wall a most splendid stained glass window. There is in itself nothing unusual about that except that it faces onto a narrow walkway and some apartment buildings that afford it relatively little of the natural light he imagined it deserved.

In late May, 2013 John Powell asked via a friend if he could see inside that building and in particular view the stained glass window. Very obligingly he was introduced to the Council's recently appointed Marketing and Development Officer, David Lawrence and allowed to do just that.

Within moments of entering the Function Room where the window is found he realised it was a mosaic of extraordinary diagrams and symbols including the representations of asterisms, icons, distributions, astronomical phenomena and much more. This was no ordinary piece of stained glass.

Once he returned home and downloaded the photographs he had taken of the window its significance became apparent. Described for 140 years as a tribute to national figures in the Arts, Science and Industry it is in fact a collection of cryptic images right out of the top drawer of mystic phenomena that the Victorians were so obsessed with.

After contacting respected historians, councillors, freemasons, long term and knowledgeable residents, archivists, newspapers and libraries it was also apparent that since its installation this window has gone undocumented and unappreciated. The extraordinary content has profound significance as a masterful contribution to the historical record of Westbury and has been utterly overlooked.

The man responsible for the astonishingly successful encrypting of information was the local Nineteenth Century industrialist and philanthropist Abraham Laverton after whom the building is named and the same man who built Prospect Square. Laverton sat as a Magistrate and represented Westbury and its district as its Member of Parliament. He held his Christian faith to be the moral fabric that sustained his values as a member of the community and the greater Victorian society and famously rejected its more acerbic social structures such as penal servitude, deportation and slavery in any context.

From the outset there have been plenty of people willing to offer advice on how to approach the task of deciphering and decoding a work of art that is multi-layered and multi-dimensional. Unfortunately most of that advice either began with 'don't do this, that or the other' or entailed tracking down someone who once knew someone who used to live near someone and so on.

It was pretty obvious that wherever possible the research process would have to be executed employing texts conforming to standards, definitions, classifications, types or any form of taxonomy that set out definitions, tables, recognised values and sources of literature. Such sources would have to set out recognised statistical criteria wherever possible. As best as I have been able to I have executed all acts of interpretation by the use of such respected sets of criteria.

For example, I have drawn upon the online resource of www.biblenews1.com for a set of rules by which all religious illustrations in stained glass were constructed.

The depth and detail of this particular analytical tool is very exhaustive. There are around seven pages dealing with little fingers and the meaning of each phalange, the direction in which each is pointing, whether it is straight or bent, if it is bent then in what shape and so on.

Given my atheistic approach to life in general I came to terms with the need to be very self-disciplined forensically acknowledging that whilst I may not agree with the most respected identifiable methodology it would give me a good comparative platform from which to launch each chapter of my investigation.

Having established one such platform it would not necessarily be the appropriate methodology for all the areas to be studied. That used for Bible based rules of interpretation would need to be different from that used in a theological line of investigation. The theology of the hands and feet in scripture belongs to the Doctrine of Creation that is not always relevant.

From a completely different perspective the appreciation of architectural features including the hidden messages in Freemason's pigpen found in the stained glass frieze of the North Transept of All Saints parish church demanded a quite different degree of knowledge and understanding. Such is to be found in books like Richard Taylor's 'How To Read a Church'. This text proved to be useful for identifying Gospels,

and Church Age in particular as well as the exact location in Farleigh Hungerford Castle where the North Transept scene is set.
Similarly, following the significance of symbols in the Window to represent everyday objects, there are plenty of resources on the Internet for appraising the significance of the clusters of acorns, the colours of flowers, the connectivity of vines, the shading of natural satellites and so on.

Nothing is proffered in this book that has not at least a reasonable academic credibility to back it up. At the same time it must be appreciated that 140 years ago most people had poor standards of literacy and it was through images and symbolism that they obtained much of their information. In that respect they were able to interpret visual data for more competently than we do today.

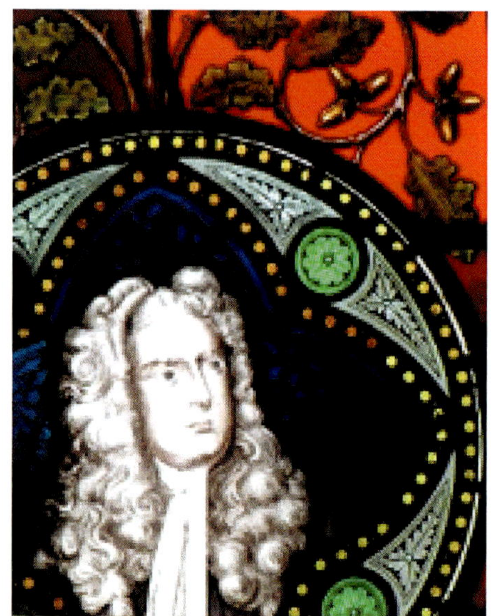

An example of the use of symbolism to convey information is seen in the second column of the Window where the head of Isaac Newton is surrounded by acorns. In Victorian Britain the acorn represented power, authority and victory from which grows new life.

The acorn was also an emblem of fidelity and often featured on gravestones and sentimentally held jewellery.

Editor's Comment

For the Editor of this book it has been an outstanding undertaking during his first year as Development and Marketing Officer for Westbury Town Council. In the year he has been living in Westbury he has been focussing outside of his defined hours of employment on completing his Open University Degree in History but this book has produced so many complimentary areas of interest that job specification has 'gone out the window'.

Personal academic and vocational commitments along with this exciting project have made every day at the Laverton a compelling challenge. Little is known of the Window. It is on record that it was installed by Horwood Bros of Frome who trained their workers in the village of Mells and were known to have constructed stained glass windows in Berkshire, Hampshire, Hertfordshire and Sussex as well as Wiltshire.

It has been an enthralling time working with John Powell and unravelling the secrets of the Window that have been hidden for 140 years. Men like Abraham Laverton led lives of extraordinary interest. He was absorbed in and committed to Rosicrucian, Templar and Masonic practices that people today have little or no understanding of and the Window is to a large extent an historical document charting his life.

Fundamental questions are not easily answered such as where does the art of the Window begin and the symbolism end? Are the clues actually there? Why did Abraham Laverton choose to target these four men? Most profoundly, why has nobody realised any this for 140 years? The Window will mean different things to different people but the book tries to guide the reader through an interpretation of the key symbols and how they impacted upon Victorian life.

Will people tend to see only what they want to? Yes, inevitably that will happen up to a point. That has been the notorious outcome for other writers in recent years. What the Window has to reveal is so much more than just a story and the reader will find the integrity of the interpretations made to be based in many places upon scientific and mathematical principles. There is something in it for everyone.

David Lawrence

Acknowledgments

There have been many people who have contributed to the production of this book not least those who have made a positive and encouraging comment at the right time when maybe I was wondering whether I was not better off doing something less demanding in my retirement.

Thanks go to Tony Truscott (and his wife Joyce) who was a critical voice for every discovery or interpretation made in researching this book. Julia Foote was immaculate in correcting the manuscript with little notice whilst David Lawrence demonstrated his multitasking skills again and again as I called for his help in researching and resourcing the text.

The staff of Westbury Town Council at the Laverton building were remarkably tolerant and generous towards my needs and my gratitude goes to Town Clerk Keith Harvey and clerical officers Barbara Mantle, Amanda McCann and Julie Dyer. The Laverton is maintained to the highest standard thanks to caretaker Richard Traynor and housekeeper Becky David making it a superb venue for events and functions and a fitting home for the Window.

My thanks go to the professional staff of the Westbury Library and the unselfish volunteers who maintain the Westbury Heritage Centre to such a high standard as well as to all the members of Westbury Lions International whose generosity of spirit is an inspiration and their charity book shop a treasure trove. I owe a big thank you to Alan Drinkwater and his staff at The Ink Shop UK in Warminster, Wilts who never once let me down in supplying all my computer needs at the drop of a hat.

The Reverend Jonathon Bourke of the Parish Church of All Saints, Westbury, Wiltshire provided a wise and willing ear to some sensitive issues that arose during my research and I am grateful to him and all his team for their selfless work.

I owe Peter Baker and his delightful wife Shirley particular thanks for helping me uncover from the dust and debris of a forgotten corner of the Parish Church some critical resources in the telling of this story. Likewise my thanks go to Nigel Coward for his much needed support.

Most notably I owe a debt of gratitude to Michael and Doreen Pearce who gave me the scent of the trail that led me to explore the meaning of the remarkable legacy left by Abraham Laverton to the people of Westbury. No finer citizens, no better place. To the remarkable Jean Lucas who came to my help yet again when most needed, diolch yn fawr.

Contents

Preface

John Powell was born in Penrhiwtyn, Neath, South Wales and raised in his early years in the Melincryddan district of that same town. His family moved later to the Lower Swansea Valley where his father worked in the iron and steel industry as had four generations of the Powell ancestry before him. The small village of Llwynbrwydraw was home to family and friends but his early education was at a school close to the city's docklands that faced out towards the picturesque Swansea Bay and the Mumbles Headland to and fro which clattered the trams of the once celebrated tramway (or railway).

At ten years of age his family moved eastwards across the South Wales coalfield to live in the Ebbw Valley where his schooling continued. Coalmining was still the dominant economic force but that traditional lifestyle was crumbling and light manufacturing was becoming the mainstay of prosperity along with the giant Llanwern Iron and Steel plant near Newport.

Having grown up in a household obsessed with sport in a country obsessed with rugby his favourite possessions from these days are a few ragged old jerseys, faded ties, early press clippings and assorted memorabilia such as music on vinyl, photographs in black and white and several teeth that are displaced trophies of foolish bravado on a sports field.

With each passing decade he became an increasingly keen traveller with Japan, Hawaii, China, Sweden, Norway, India, Australia, Tanzania and Arizona amongst his fondest places visited. As he grew older his interests and pastimes changed from ball sports, scuba diving, pot holing, trekking, motorcycling and swimming to lecturing in local history, astronomy, playing chess, doing crossword puzzles, running marathons, gardening and DIY.

Whatever the levels of talents he had for any of these things they provided him with the skills sets that allowed him to understand what Abraham Laverton was doing when he paid for an elaborate stained glass window to be installed in the building named after himself in the town of Westbury, Wiltshire in 1873.

There is no evidence that anyone has metaphorically or literally seen through the amazing codes, ciphers, symbols, diagrams, mathematics, ambiguous items of art, contradictions, innuendos or red herrings that are unchallenged in 140 years. It is intended that the erudite people of Westbury become aware as soon as possible of their extraordinary civic possession and its unique qualities.

The town of Westbury is situated in the rural heart of the county of Wiltshire in the West of England. From its eastern margins rise the expanse of Salisbury Plain the west facing escarpment of which is marked by the splendid White Horse of Westbury, a relief sculpture carved into the chalk landscape that is a landmark for miles around.

Westbury has an ancient recorded history that notes the extensive hill fort above the town as a defensive feature resorted to by successive Kings of Wessex particularly Alfred the Great who defeated the Danes in the year 878 A.D., two centuries before its mention in the Domesday Book in 1086. At the heart of the civil parish of Westbury is the fourteenth century Parish Church of All Saints that houses the third heaviest ring of bells in the world, an Erasmus Bible and a clock that has no face. Both the east and west walls contain magnificent stained glass windows and others of equal quality but smaller are to be admired throughout the edifices of the Church.

During the last two centuries two things have especially shaped the fortunes of the town, the coming of the railways and the rise of the once thriving woollen mills. Both of these played major parts in the fortunes of Abraham Laverton and how he rose from being an ordinary country boy to being an outstanding entrepreneur and man of the people.

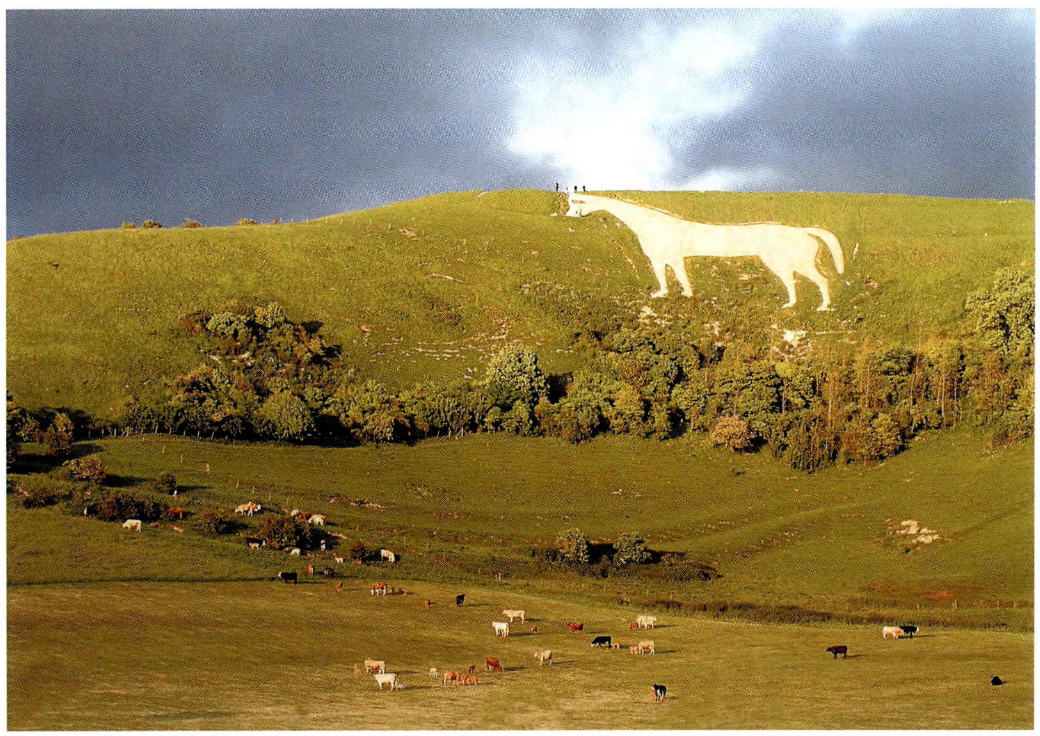

The Westbury White Horse

Today Westbury's population is increasing as the Town grows as a dormitory settlement for commuters working in Bath and Salisbury and as a commercial centre in its own right. John Powell came to live in Westbury, Wiltshire for that reason and after five years commuting daily 30 miles to and fro The Stonehenge School in Amesbury he retired from a most enjoyable, professional life in which the pupils he taught were as second to none.

In his retirement he has discovered a West Country world very different from anything he has previously experienced. Older people talk intimately about their upbringings in a place that was fashioned by woollen mills and railways but set in an agricultural tradition of sheep farming, living from the land, chaff cutters and ox ploughs, thatched roofs and cat skin rugs, mole skin waistcoats and corduroy kitsch, truffle hunting and cock fighting, bacon pudding and lardy cake, scrap iron higglers and pig jobbers.

In fact, he has encountered a veritable dictionary of terms that go beyond mere colloquialism or turn of phrase and amount to a language rather than a dialect.

In that time of learning he has watched from his home in the summer evenings the remarkable spectacle of the setting sun in midsummer upon the houses of Prospect Square, a residential precinct close to where he lives. Every bit as alien as the local linguistics is the manipulation of light upon the facades of these houses in a manner he has not seen before.

These houses were built by Abraham Laverton and designed by William Jervis Stent. Stent had a namesake and close relative who lived and worked as a glazier in the nearby town of Frome. Between the three of them they colluded to create not only the visual extravaganza of Prospect Square but also the masterpiece of their lives in the form of the Westbury Window upon which this book focuses.

If anyone should visit the Window at the Laverton building it is germane to consider the limitations of the human eye and seeing the Window close up is to view it in one dimension. As will be demonstrated it is multi-dimensional and a challenge even to visualise what Abraham Laverton was trying to represent. Hopefully this book will help to achieve that.

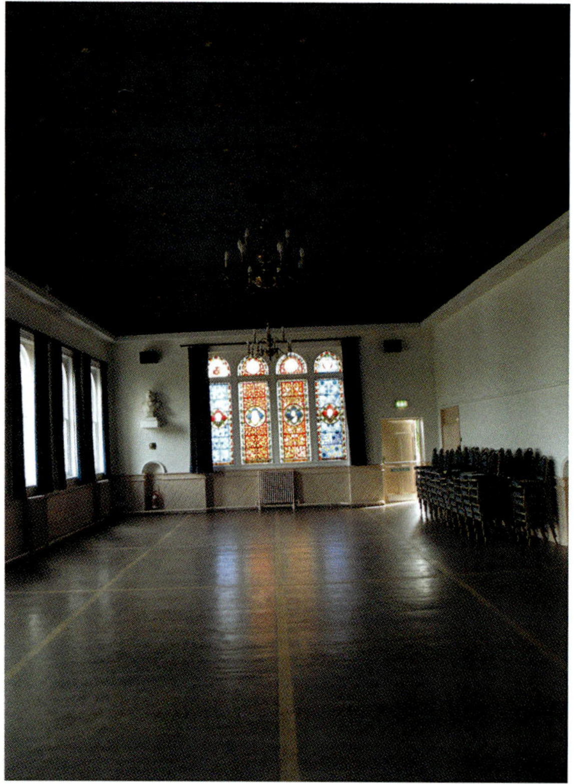

In the East Wall (facing) may be seen the Window

Chapter 1
Introduction

The name Abraham Laverton is recognised in Westbury by every man, woman or child above a modest age of cognizance as belonging to a giant of entrepreneurial achievement during the Nineteenth Century. The people of the town are informed at an early age that this man was a role model for philanthropic benevolence, served his community as a JP and represented his town and country as an MP.

Abraham Laverton founded woollen mills that employed hundreds of the townsfolk for decades, sponsored the construction of a number of railway companies, invested in gas and iron works for the town, established brick, tile and pottery works and promoted the consolidation of small farms in the district. As former Mayor of Westbury Mike Pearce says:

> He probably did more for Westbury than anyone else in history. He embraced the new technologies of his age, cared for his workers in the style of Robert Owen, represented the best interests of the citizens in a myriad of public forums and set standards of religious devotion and principle that all could aspire to.

Laverton understood deeply the relationship between the Protestant Ethic and the Spirit of Capitalism propounded by the likes of Max Weber and that made him focused and successful in his time but he also appreciated that those who relied upon him for their subsistence had rights, deserved a consideration of fair play and opportunity and should always have their integrity respected. Today Councillor Gordon King believes that the people of Westbury:

> virtually carry in their DNA a consideration for their fellow man that is based upon exercising common decency and fair play. All my life in this Town I have lived amongst good people.

That is Laverton's legacy. He established a manufacturing foundation for the local economy to grow and prosper from and did so in a fashion that engendered a community spirit, esprit de corps and an awareness that when each of us slips off this mortal coil we will need to answer to a higher authority. As material evidence of his walking the walk in 1869 he completed the spending of a large amount of company profits building the residences of Prospect Square, a three sided rectangular collection of dwellings for his workers that conformed to standards of architectural and domestic excellence not provided before in the Town for the common man

He built for the people at considerable expense what became known as, and still is, the Laverton Building, more correctly designated the Laverton Institute, completed in 1873 with the purpose - as Anthony Laverton writes in the biography of his ancestor titled "Abraham Laverton JP MP 1819 to 1886: the rise and rise of a Westbury Woollen Mill Owner" - of providing

> a place for religious, educational, literary, scientific, philanthropic and political purpose.

Anthony Laverton continues,

> A large stained glass window dedicated to Industry and the Arts dominates one end of the building. The four main panes from left to right depict William Shakespeare, Isaac Newton, James Watt and Sir Edwin Landseer. Across the top can be seen Abraham's coat of arms on the left and Westbury's on the right separated by two legends: 'Industry brings wealth' and 'Knowledge is Power'.

He continues in another sentence or two to summarise the content of the imagery in the stained glass.

It seems to be the case that since its installation exactly 140 years ago that has been the height of all that has been written about it. Since 1873 'The Laverton' has hosted thousands of council meetings, weddings receptions, concerts, lectures, conferences and scores of other community activities to a footfall of millions. In that time the window has been justly admired and Abraham Laverton justly lauded for what he was, a great man and a good man.

However, Abraham Laverton was also an extremely clever man and has successfully hoodwinked his contemporaries and their descendants right up to the present day. Academics, Artisans and the 'apathetic' alike have failed to 'see through the window' and the cryptic imagery it contains. Not only have the mindless stone throwers who have abused the window in the past been defeated but generations have been confounded.

This book is a first step in setting the record straight and revealing some of the meanings of the remarkable imagery and symbolism it contains.

It should first be noted that the window was obviously not the creation of one man. Laverton paid for it and doubtless dictated what its content would be but his architect for both Prospect Square and the Window was one William Jervis Stent and he was clearly of no mean intellect too. They respectively owned brick, tile and pottery companies in Westbury and neighbouring Warminster and must surely have colluded to have created such a graphic conundrum.

The window is approximately three metres high by three metres wide and on first encounter is very impressive though not awe inspiring. The first striking features are the 'head shots' of Shakespeare, Newton, Watt and Landseer that are of the highest quality and for which no expense was spared. For example, it is thought that Shakespeare's head is taken from the picture known as the Chandos portrait housed in the National Portrait Gallery in London. It would, in the artistic environment of such a time, have commanded a sterling premium to replicate.

The image of James Watt is even more impressive having been copied from the bust (or a likeness of that bust) of the great man as sculptured by Sir Frances Leggatt Chantrey, a phenomenally talented artist whose surname is to be found for a walkway in Westbury today close to the site of Abraham Laverton's former Angel Mill.

These personages are for most people viewing the Window what catches their attention and what they remember when they have gone. In truth Abraham Laverton was a complex character and as we shall learn he did not celebrate these men but pillory them for their unprincipled exploitation of their fellow man. Over and above their faces oozes a stellar mix of symbolic damnation, iconic contempt and uncompromising judgement. Ultimately there is indifference as the dimensions of the Window transmutate to serve their prime purposes as the alchemists' data recorder, the astronomer's celestial plane and a multimedia vehicle for his spiritual return to his beloved Westbury.

Added to the above sample of considerations are a difficult series of abstract concepts such as mythical status, normalisation, implicitness and truth. These underlay finer points but do not lend themselves to quantitative assessment (e.g. simple correlation). Neither do the distributions of stars and other celestial objects in the asterisms and constellations of the four stained glass columns.

Confidence in my recognition of Ursa Major, Orion, Andromeda and the Pleiades is a result of my taking my ideas to expert clinicians in astronomical practise such as local industrialist Nigel Coward. Nigel is a highly intelligent and very competent astronomer who in the early days of my investigations concurred unequivocally with my recognition of Ursa Major and supported then my ongoing analyses of the other three asterisms.

To appreciate the configuration of the asterisms in the Window is to begin to see one layer of the Window's make-up. To fail to see any one of them is to fail to understand the fundamentals of the graphicacy employed. To state that picturing these features of the night sky is a matter of interpretation can only be seen as poor understanding and an intellectual shortcoming.

By far the most complex consideration in the study of this Window is the consideration of the data dealing with the eclipse phenomena. With regard to this aspect of the Window there is to be revealed in due course some jaw dropping revelations that will require a level of mathematical ability above and beyond basic competency.

Chapter 2
Alignments

Each year I have lived in Westbury I have observed the extraordinary light show that takes place in Prospect Square that is a residential precinct built on a steep hill situated between my home and the Town Centre of Westbury. For the 6 to 8 weeks or so either side of Midsummer's day the setting sun (when it can be seen) is spectacularly reflected and refracted from the tiled surfaces of house facades on the northern side of the Square.

A fall of rain or heavy dew is enough to provide quite intense reflections as the houses light up one by one from the bottom of the hill upwards. The last two are always the best and if there has been a shower of rain the show is a spectacular one. Surprisingly, few Westbury residents have noticed this and blank reactions often prevail when it is mentioned suggesting the same unknowing that has gone hand in hand with the lost awareness of the Window.

Only the most spectacular photographs and personal encounters with the phenomenon have generally imparted some interest. There is something in the human psyche that is attracted to order and alignment. The Stonehenge monument some 20 miles away and all that it is associated with is an obvious example on a macro level. On a more personalised level the concept of lay lines popularised in this country by Alfred Watkins in the early 1920s attracts a different kind of expectation. The former seems to have cosmic implications whilst the latter is bound to landscape features and the patterns of man's development.

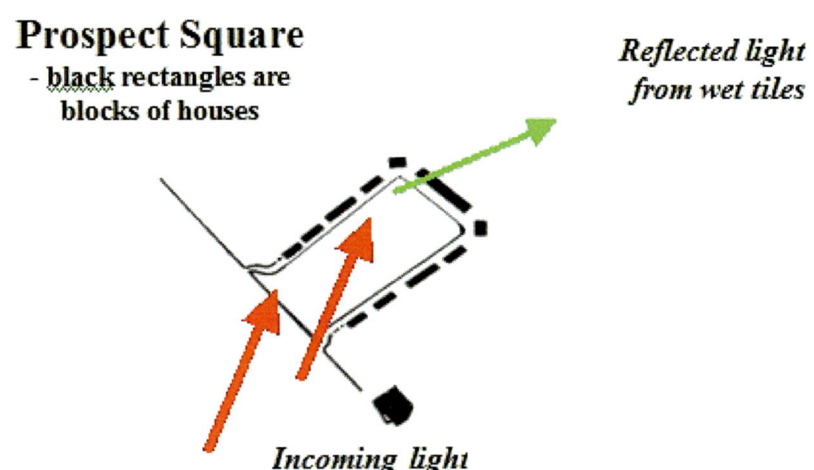

The sketch diagram above illustrates the direction of light at sunset as it reflects off the south west facing houses of Prospect Square, Westbury

Lines link the two and transcend them. Abraham Laverton and William Jervis Stent had perceptions of linear patterns in time and space that most people are never aware of or maybe cannot be bothered with, or maybe do not understand.

Both men arrived at the patch of land that was to become the residential area of Prospect Square in Westbury from differing career paths, one the entrepreneur, businessman, philanthropist, politician and the other an architect, industrialist and developer. What they shared was a common mind to construct in their building of Prospect Square something that exercised their intellects as well as their architectural nous. They decided to give the occupants of the new designer dwellings (the specifications of which far exceeded the expectations of the average factory worker) a free light show through the weeks of midsummer every year ad infinitum.

Unfortunately, the quality of the environmental setting of the Square has been dealt with unsympathetically by architects and planners over the last fifty years. This contrasts with cities like Lyons in France where a whole culture has built up around the reflectivity of buildings and that city has a festival of light every year to exhibit just that. In the 2012 celebrations of the Queen's Diamond Jubilee the front of Buckingham Palace was used as a giant projection screen by the band called Madness with great success. The light directions in the Prospect Square phenomenon that first caught John Powell's attention and are shown below.

As the reflectivity fades on the lower houses so the upper houses become more radiant. Careful viewing of the first photograph allows the viewer to see quite extensive reflections.

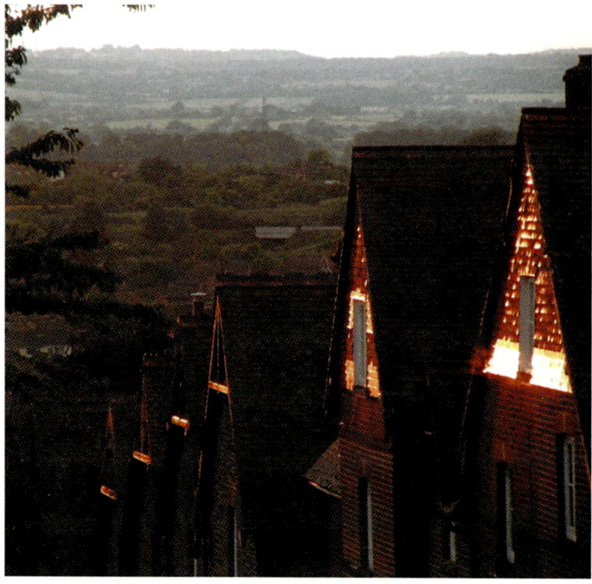 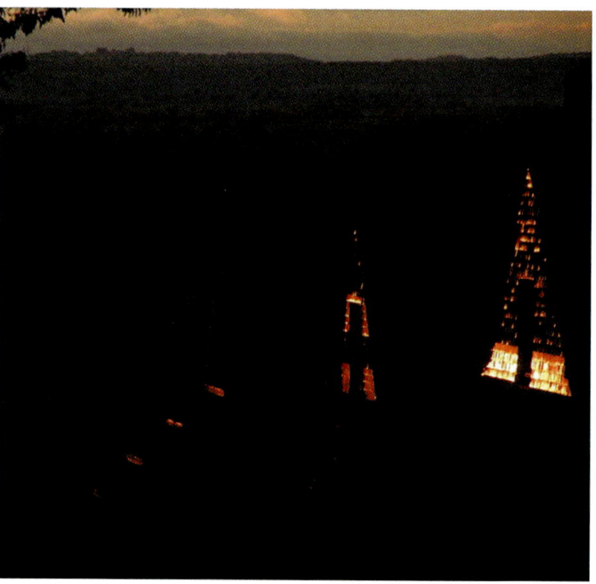

As the sun disappears darkness falls and the lightshow is at its best. If Abraham Laverton had a shortcoming it was his lack of foresight regarding how the landscape of his mid-Victorian world would change with time.

The patterns of reflectivity have been greatly interrupted by the growth of trees in the Square and the facades of houses on the lower south facing slope do not see the sun as was intended.

As a trainee, student or apprentice of architecture Stent would have learned that a fundamental principle of his professional practice is to always know what light sources do to his intended structures. In the case of Prospect Square the response of Stent was to produce a visual lesson in how certain materials may be used to literally brighten the lives of people. Unfortunately all is not as it once was.

Prospect Square offers up a good example of why the Laverton Stained Glass Window has been overlooked as an architectural feature that should be lauded as an art work and used as a resource to promote tourism in the Town and its district, enhance the educational programmes of schools in the area and stimulate civic pride.

Similarly the line of the sun rising in midsummer used to shine though the Stained Glass Window of the Laverton building. It has now been interrupted by new buildings, fences, and trees. The original context is lost.

At a time when living standards were rising but the cost of living was rising even faster these houses were prized.

Just as there are natural astronomical alignments such as eclipses, conjunctions, neaps or highs that effect our planet so there are man-made alignments that may or may not have some useful function. One of the most common type of alignment is that pandering to the vanity of a ruler. Any book about politics in Nineteenth Century Britain may be illustrated by examples of a dynastic power organising lines of infrastructure for its own convenience first and that of its local population as an afterthought.

With regard to anything along those lines Abraham Laverton's integrity is beyond reproach but he did do something extraordinary. The Laverton Institute building as measured by David Lawrence and me, is aligned in an aspect with its stained glass window facing 68 degrees east of north. One might imagine this is the angle of the rising sun on midsummer's day or something of similar astral significance.

It is in fact a straight co-ordinate that bisects the Laverton Function Room and if followed over the rise of an intervening hill from the middle of the Stained Glass Window it extends to bisect almost exactly the graveyard on the Bratton Road where Abraham Laverton is buried. Thirteen years before he died in 1886 he seems to have had his future well in order. The sketch map following shows this.

Abraham Laverton's grave is not a splendid tribute to the skills of the stonemason but a quite modest burial plot for such a rich man. The key feature is the 'Celtic Cross' that is at the head of the grave. The gravestone is squat in its' structure but as noted it is lined up in the same direction as others. There is little making it stand out unless one pays more attention to size or until it is appreciated that it is not a Celtic cross as popularly referred to.

In an outstandingly well maintained cemetery the grass on the Laverton plot was slightly long but any difficulty in reading the monument's inscription was because of the poor relief and/or weathering of the stone. (See below)

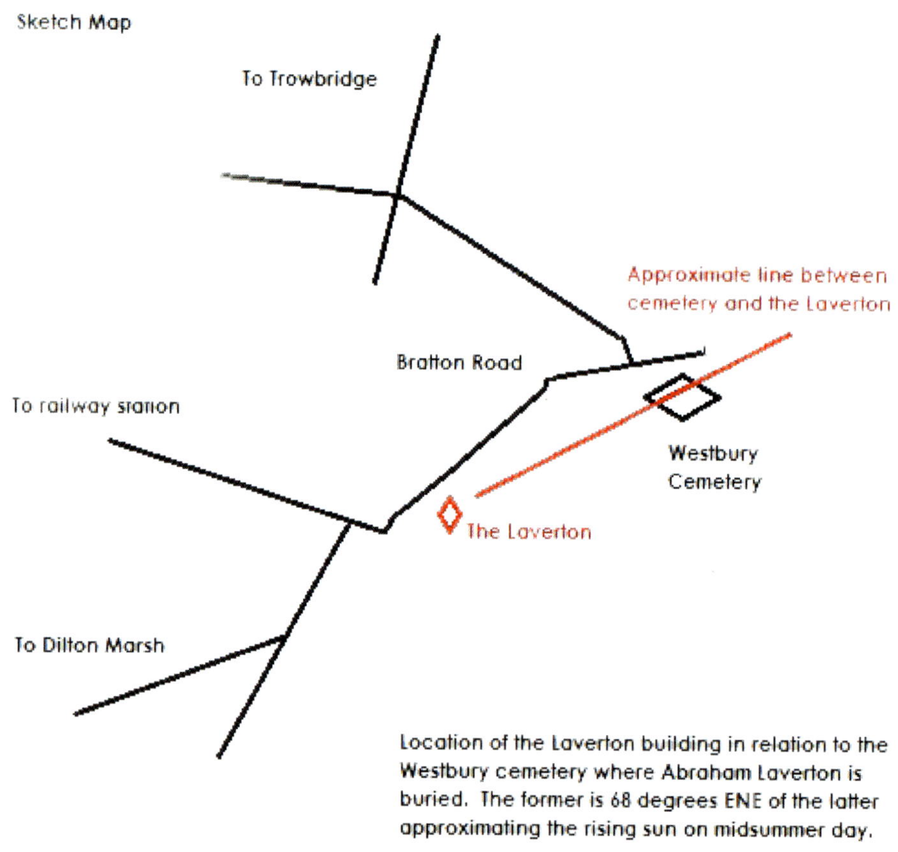

Location of the Laverton building in relation to the Westbury cemetery where Abraham Laverton is buried. The former is 68 degrees ENE of the latter approximating the rising sun on midsummer day.

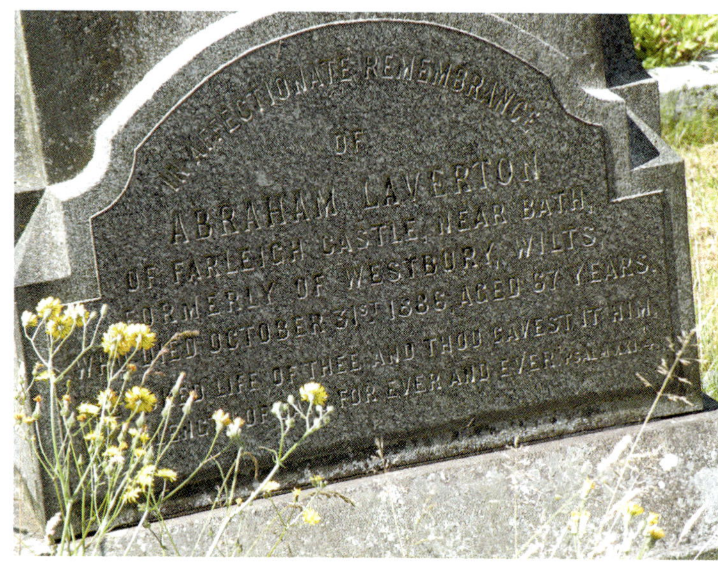

Abraham Laverton's headstone.

The text on the monument reads as follows, the best that I can make out:

IN AFFECTIONATE REMEMBRANCE OF ABRAHAM LAVERTON OF FARLEIGH CASTLE NEAR BATH FORMERLY OF WESTBURY WILTS DIED OCTOBER 31ST 1886 AGED 67 YEARS. HE ASKED LIFE OF THEE AND THOU GIVEST IT HIM EVEN LENGTH OF DAYS FOR EVER AND EVER.

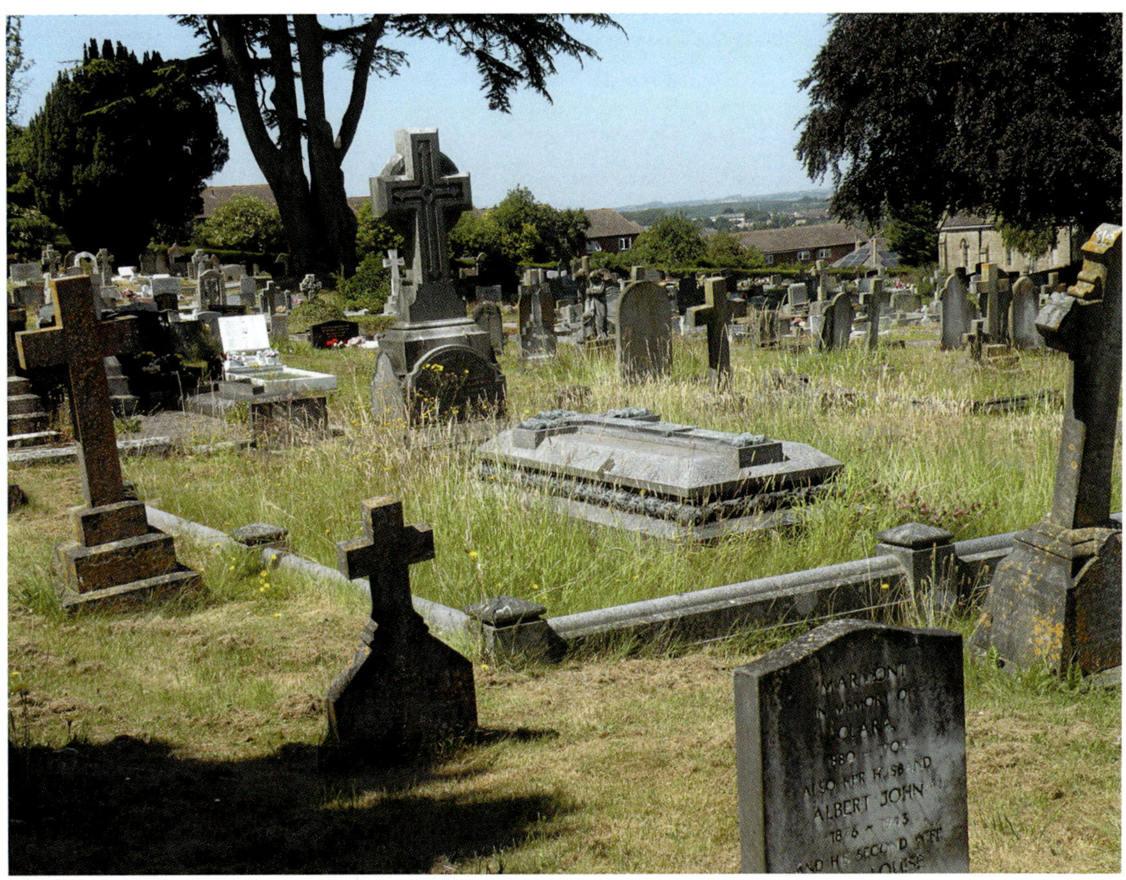

The last sentence is a quote from the Bible, Psalms 21:4 and has the popular interpretation that the deceased is to be with Jesus, ever living or as St Augustine may have stated 'for eternity, world without end'. This was in every way Laverton's ambition on Earth and what he spent his latter years dedicated to. (Above, the Laverton burial plot)

The concept of these alignments is ultimately determined by the Christian tradition that places of worship and the dead that they bury face the East. The religious principle here stems from the Latin 'ad orientum' that is the practise of acknowledging the rising sun itself a symbol of the 'universality of God'.

In the Catholic Church this requires the priest to conduct the Mass with his back to the people. This is somewhat ironic when few churches in this country face due east anyhow. Abraham Laverton would have seen such irony for what it is. What is often referred to as the Celtic Cross above Laverton's grave is (for those who have not guessed already) a Rosy Cross.

Chapter 3
Configuration, Composition and Content

a)   Mapping the content of the window

The window is a complex structure and it is necessary to have some kind of reference framework in order to accurately identify any feature in the design. I include the following referral key for that purpose into which any referral may be made.
- 4 columns
- each column is divided into an upper light, main panels and a centre inset
- each upper light is divided into an outer rim, an inner rim, a main image and a surround.
- main panels in each column are divided into 12 units numbered 1 to 12.
- Each centre inset is divided into inner portrait and outer rim

At the bottom of each column is the base rim.

Appendix 2 at the end of this book contains a sample outline for four columns and may be copied freely by the purchaser of this book

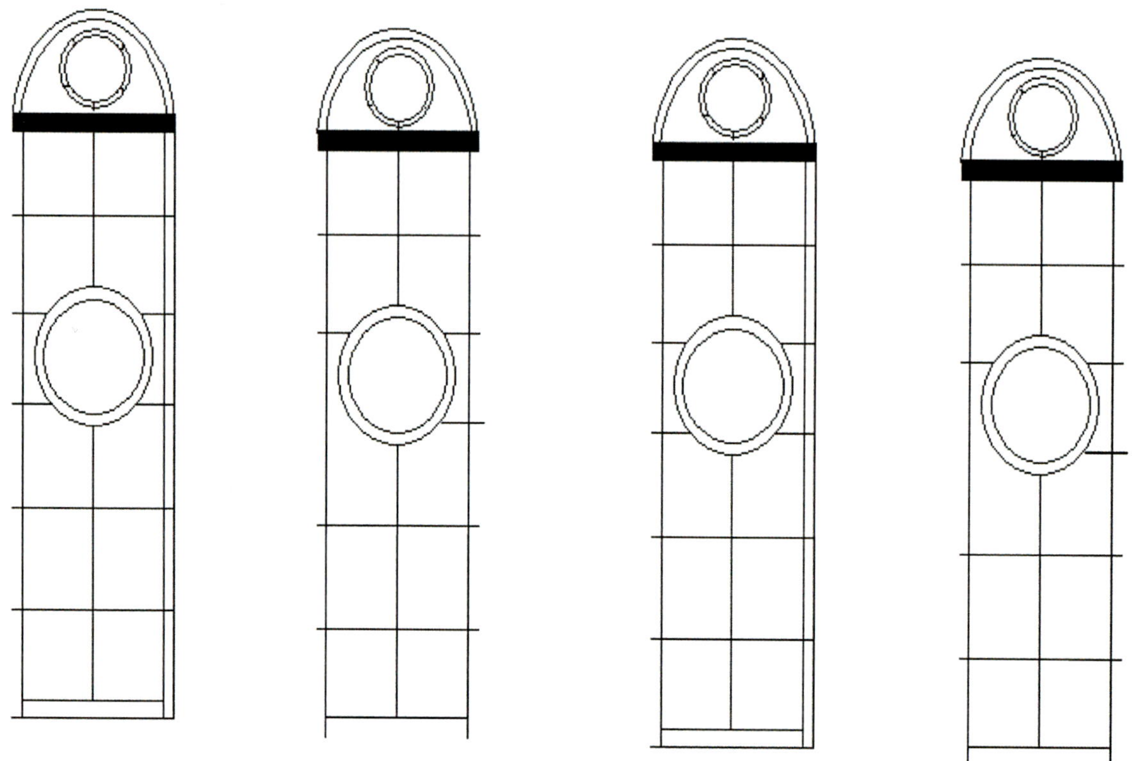

Sketch diagram for identifying main panels in stained glass units

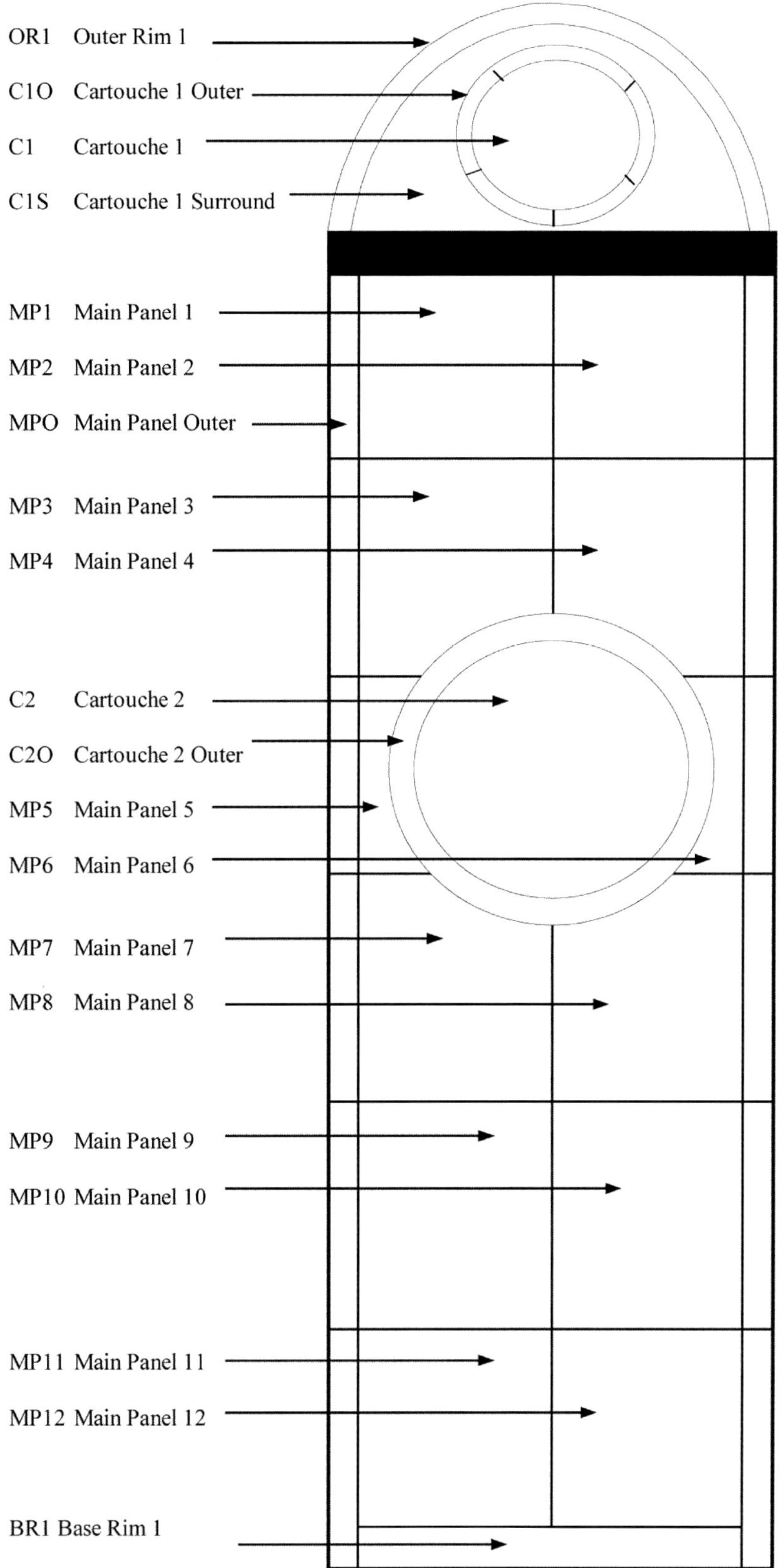

*Sketch diagram of key to identifying panels
in the Westbury Window*

b)   Stained Glass

The manufacture of objects made from stained glass dates back to the early Egyptians and the Phoenicians for whom it was a prized possession. Places such as Antioch and Tyre were specifically associated with early objects and by the time when the Roman Empire was at its most powerful the ownership of stained glass had become a status symbol.

The Lycurgus Cup held in the British Museum in London is a celebrated early object as is the Portland vase but in Europe stained glass has always been more associated with the windows of churches, monasteries and buildings of public importance. As early as the Seventh century there are records of skilled craftsmen in the making of stained glass travelling from mainland Europe to the north of England to glaze windows.

Equally there is a Muslim tradition of making the finest stained glass in countries like Syria where Damascus and Aleppo produced gilded glass that was similarly popular. Here the same traditional skills of mixing pigments and fusing coloured metallic oxides into glass or the painting and 'baking' of transparent colours onto a glass surface were honed.

In the eighth century a Persian chemist known as Geber listed scores of formulae for producing specific colours from specific metals. He realised that it was the oxide of a metal that coloured any glass and as a result vast arrays of colours were made possible. Ironically Geber also learned from his work that many colours were damaged by prolonged exposure to sunlight some darkening to be opaque whilst others faded away.

Examples of metals that impart colours on to glass include –
Selenium oxide   red
Antimony oxides   white
Lead compounds   yellow
Cobalt oxide   blue
Carbon oxides   amber brown
Uranium oxides   fluorescent yellow
Nickel oxide   violet

In the use of stained glass for windows it is coloured the same way using metallic compounds but its shape will have been fashioned according to need. Frameworks will have been made almost exclusively by shaping lead strips to form meaningful patterns and a mosaic style picture. Whole 'lights' will consist of many small pieces of stained glass that illuminate when viewed against a light source.

In Christian churches there is a tradition of incorporating narratives from biblical sources such as the stations-of-the-cross. Historical statements carry more weight in this context as to a far greater extent do hagiographic images or armorial symbolic motifs. The Westbury Window has some very precise design features in its stained glass that will be discussed at length.

c)   The Content of the Westbury Window

The Westbury Window found in the east wall of the Function Room of the Laverton Institute building is a complex design but may be broken down in the following way. This is not the only way to consider it but it is a structure to begin with.

Firstly there are the four images of the representatives of the arts and sciences that the window ostensibly was set up to pay tribute to; Shakespeare, Newton, Watt and Landseer.

Secondly there are the four columns of twelve panes of glass plus borders that surround those four images and contain vine-like structures that have different types of flower or fruit. These make up shapes and patterns of asterisms (that are parts of constellations in the night sky) that for some reasons are associated with the four men of the arts and sciences.

Thirdly at the top of each of the columns of stained glass there are semi-circular headers. Respectively they illustrate (from left to right) Abraham Laverton's personal crest or coat of arms, an industrial scene, Watt's locomotive and the former Westbury Town coat of arms. All four carry mottoes, the first and last being in Latin.

Fourthly, there runs through all four sets of the aforementioned, graphic data-streams relating to the phenomena of solar and lunar eclipses.

Fifthly there are speculative reasons for suggesting that the data streams are associated with ancient systems for measuring time and, according to the ancient Chaldeans, life expectancy.

Sixthly there is the stunningly brilliant composite aspiration of Abraham Laverton to create the ultimate cosmic experience.

Themes of astrology run throughout the design but without a single structure or area of placement. Colour is used meaningfully but is too complex to consider in this book. The linear patterns of vines in the columns are clearly associated with the Freemasons as are the encrypted messages in the Laverton stained glass in the All Saints Parish Church, Westbury. The influence of the Knights Templar occurs throughout the Window whilst their coding and criteria for symbolic representations is fundamental to 'reading' the Window.

With these things in mind the viewer looking at the Window must then consider the dimensions in which the Window is set. The four basic mathematical or scientific dimensions are length, breadth (or width), height and time.

There is a fifth dimensional concept that the viewer is required to grasp and that is "reflection" because if the main vertical sets of panes in the columns of the Window are looked at carefully they are seen to be mirror images of each other. If they can then be imagined to be folded into each other they form third dimensional 'pop ups' like a child's picture book with an extra relief or depth.

However, this may be considered looking out through the Window or looking in giving that 'pop up' folded dimension in both directions. As light travels in both of those directions and transversally through the cross plane of the 'pop ups' this makes for a need for flexible thought when looking at the Window.

In addition to that the viewer must appreciate that the Window is an overwritten palimpsest of information. Overwriting was something the literate classes of Victorian England did without thinking. If someone wrote a letter and ran out of paper in doing so they turned the paper 90 degrees and wrote over the top of what they had already written. What they had on paper when they finished might seem to today's reader a crisscrossed jumble and impossible to read but they were used to it and took it in their visual stride.

Remarkably they might even turn their precious sheet of paper 90 degrees for a second time (or maybe 45 degrees) and continue writing. The resulting document today might be thought to be surely incomprehensible but not so. Just as paper resources were precious so were the canvases of artists. Rarely would a canvas used by a painter be used only once. As an expensive overhead a canvas might have been 'cleaned' and reused any number of times. Traces of earlier works or even complete earlier works might be painted over only to be discovered by say a restorer years later. Such a canvas is called a palimpsest.

The basic resource material that Abraham Laverton had to work with was glass and he did not use it cheaply. It will be described in this book how the elaborate artwork in the beautiful stained glass was conceived to portray information on at least three levels over and above the mathematical dimensions of the physical unit.

The superficial level may be seen in the pretty green rosettes that form a square around the prominences behind each of the personages. On a macro level these rosettes represent the stages of the Moon in its 28 day cycle between total brightness and total darkness as well as its periodicity in the event of an eclipse. On a micro level Laverton the alchemist uses those same rosettes to represent the stages in the Rotation of the Elements that was a key process in the sublimation of chemicals substances that he practised in his 'scientific' research.

Everything in the Window has multiple significances and anyone who looks at the image of an acorn and thinks it is just an acorn must think again, and again. In the abstract areas of philanthropy, philosophy, theocracy, theosophy, symbolism and cryptography the vagaries of subjectivity and interpretation are enough of a hindrance. It is a demanding Window to look through.

Chapter 4
William Shakespeare: Damnation or Salvation?

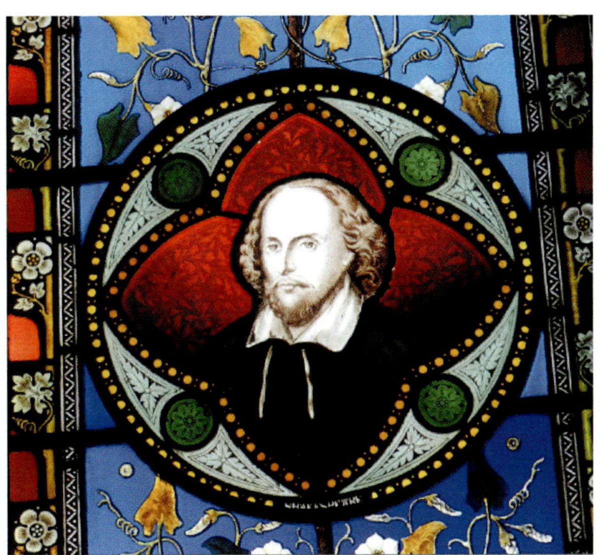

When the Laverton Institute building was opened in Westbury in 1873 it was Abraham Laverton's philanthropic intention to promote life opportunities for the population of Westbury and its young men in particular. He had achieved great wealth himself by making the most of his God-given talent and his honest endeavour. He would not have tolerated timewasters or charlatans and saw through such people.

The stained glass window in the Laverton building was publicised as a tribute to four of the great Britons who had in the Victorian era or before contributed outstandingly to the arts or sciences. These were William Shakespeare, Isaac Newton, James Watt and Edwin Landseer. In fact, nothing could be further from the truth with regard to Abraham Laverton's attitude towards these men. Far from being celebrated this men are set up to be pilloried.

Laverton was contemptuous of all four men and the inclusion of their images in the window is their public humiliation. To a large extent Laverton was venting his spleen and holding them up to public ridicule. In Shakespeare's case (as Laverton saw it) his dishonesty in claiming to have produced plays and poems that were the work of others made him deserving of harsh criticism, even damnation!

Laverton was riding on a fashionable bandwagon of public condemnation of the Bard fuelled by a belief that he had been mimicking the endeavour of others. Supporters of this standpoint justified their writings in newspapers, periodicals and other popular literature. Laverton's public ridicule of three of the men paled with the degree of contempt shown towards Landseer.

Of course the great irony has turned out to be that in the 140 years the window has been in situ of the millions of people who have looked at it there is no record of anyone seeing the scores of coded images, ciphers, double meanings or inversions.

This book cannot tell the full story as my mathematics is not good enough but may be used to get the essential information into the public domain around Spring 2014. The reader must firstly have an appreciation of the importance of symbolic data, pictorial representation and graphicacy for the average Victorian.

Such appreciation may be realised easily if books like Al Seckel's *'Incredible Visual Illusions'* are considered even briefly. Adults and children in this country were largely illiterate in the 1860s and 1870s and cartoon style drawings or sketches had great influence upon their opinions and values. False representations or tricks played in the drafting of such images were a way of life.

It was often done for political reasons but was also done for social and educational purposes amongst others. Victorian Britain was full of examples of how the human mind is fooled by unexpected visual data and in this instance if the image of Shakespeare is turned upside down there is clearly the head of a goat integrated into the face of the playwright.

The goat typically represents the Devil in much literature and art produced since the 16th or 17th centuries but for many more hundreds of years before that the goat represented 'damnation' and my best guess would be that Abraham Laverton is damning Shakespeare in his afterlife to an eternity where he will be distanced from his Lord and Maker and suffer appropriately.

This seems harsh but Laverton was an idealist and a perfectionist. The kind of fraud he seems to have believed Shakespeare to be guilty of obviously distressed him. The implications are that people were damning the Bard for centuries before that and even in his own lifetime. When out of curiosity I looked at the Chandos portrait of Shakespeare held at the National Portrait Gallery the same goat or his twin is in that too.

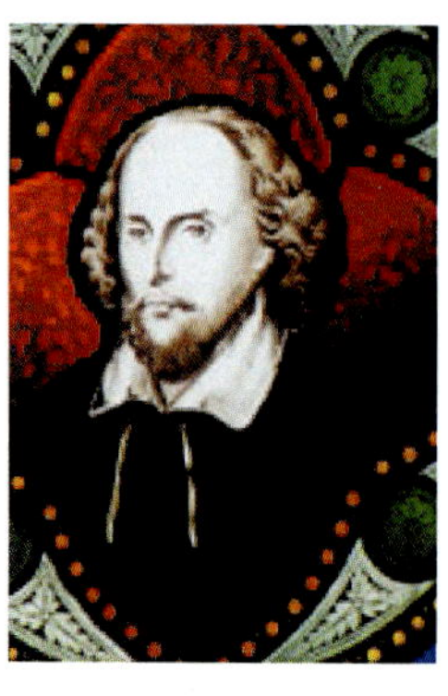

1

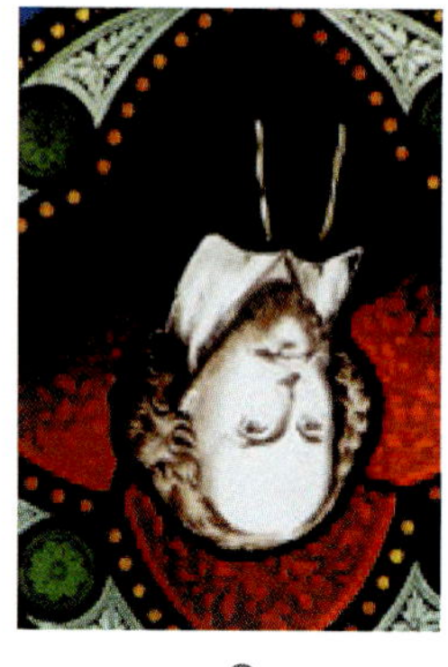

2

The Chandos Shakespeare portrait was an engraving by a man named John Taylor and thought also to be the only likeness of Shakespeare for which he may have sat and the only one made of him during his lifetime. It is a poor-quality picture and if somebody was sold such an object today they might consider asking for their money back.

It is largely dark greys and black and Shakespeare looks a decidedly shifty character but in their universal numbering system at the NPG it is Number 1, their very first acquisition on 2nd December 1856.

To see this goat initially takes a bit of effort but as with many such illusions once seen it cannot be ignored. The reader is not meant to be looking for an Ansel Adams masterpiece. The issue is one of symbolism and an image or images that are symbolic of a goat. Above there is the Westbury Window image of Shakespeare and secondly of it turned upside down.

The semblance of the goat may be seen below. I have simply cropped the images and after feeble efforts to trace the goat I have realised that my artwork will never win a gold rosette. So let the readers judge for themselves whether there is a cropped goat on show.

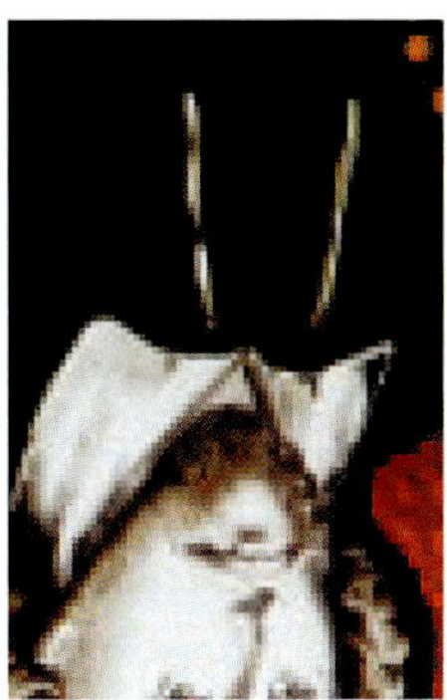

The goat is to be seen in the upside down Shakespeare as consisting of –

1. The tassles hanging from Shakespeare's collars being its horns
2. Its ears being at right angle to its horns and protruding to the left and right of its head. Hair from its ears hangs downwards.
3. Its nose is the shadow of Shakespeare's lower lip.
4. Its mouth is Shakespeare's mouth.
5. There is a band of brown hair across its head and over its eyes that the correct way up is Shakespeare's beard.

Each of these features is indicated below. For anyone doubting this goat's provenance as a goat they may simply use their own PC search engine to find images of goats on the Net and doppelgangers galore are herded on screen.

I suspected it would be in the Chandos portrait too, and appears to be so. It is not as clear as the Westbury image of a goat (not that that is clear) but having looked at many of these creatures in the results of search engine enquiries it is an above average image. It does lack detail but the Chandos image is itself a murky engraving that scores of artists have used to produce their own fanciful paintings of the playwright and poet without ever having set eyes on him or even been alive at the same time.

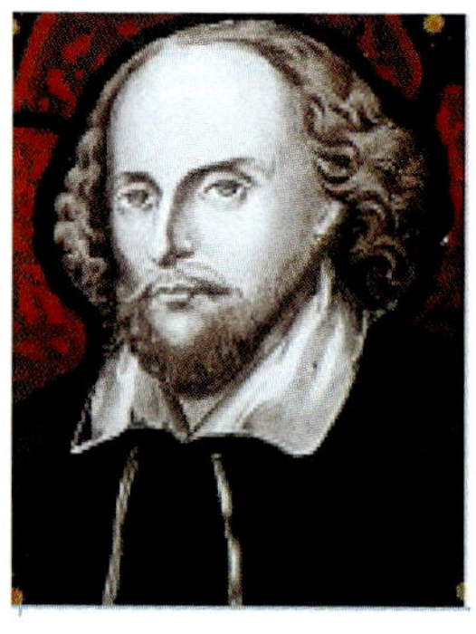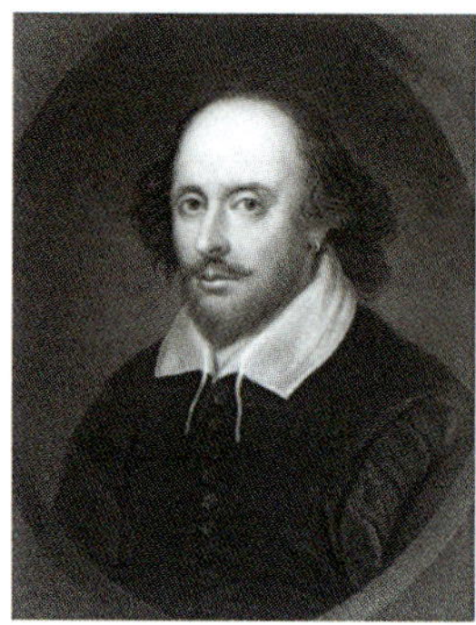

Images of Shakespeare from the Westbury Window and a royalty-free Chandos look-a-like portrait substitute. The five selected features of the look-a-like closely match both the Westbury and the Chandos portraits providing a very useful tool for comparisons.

The first impression I had when the two images were scaled and placed adjacent taking care not to disproportion the integrity of any adjustments was that the images had a common outline. I selected five common reference points:

1. where hairlines meets partings.
2. Earrings.
3. line between lips'
4. shoulders of jacket. meets collar.
5. where left and right collars of jackets meet.

These features were lined along horizontal references and emerged as being near identical. Unfortunately copyright restrictions prevent me from showing this but anyone is free to search it for themselves on the Internet. Here a mock image drawn by myself structured around four of those five lines of integrity is shown with the Westbury Window image. Being in the public domain it has presently no such constraints.

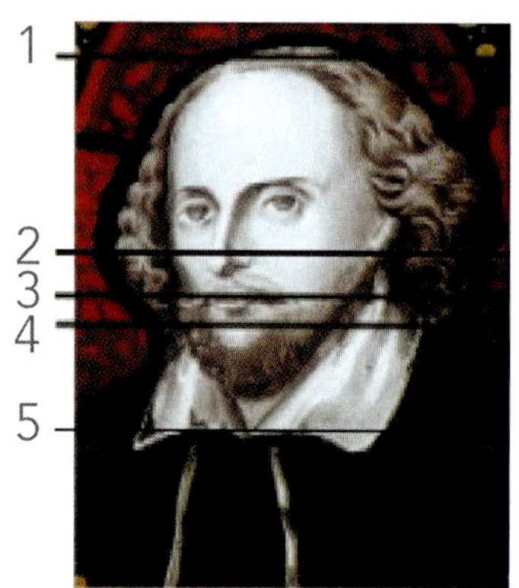

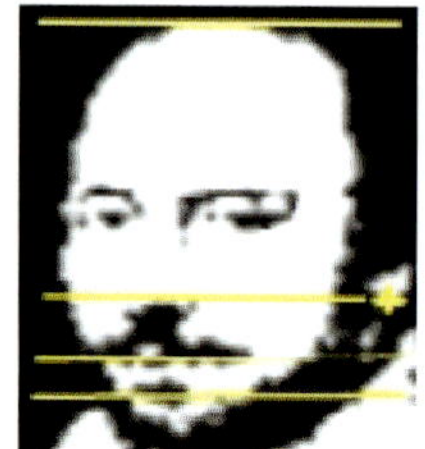

Comparison of features along horizontal lines

Another comparative exercise I carried out was to trace the outline of the Westbury Shakespeare and at the same scale see how well it fits the Chandos Shakespeare. The result was one of extraordinary similarity. The trace led to a number of tentative deductions:

- The Chandos and Westbury images are sourced from the same portrait.
- That portrait is probably the Chandos engraving. The accuracy of one against the other suggests the artist of the Westbury Shakespeare had very accurate source material or an intimate knowledge of the Chandos portrait.

- If the viewer of the Chandos portrait knows what to look for the basic outline of the goat is there to see and is not difficult when the Westbury Shakespeare is seen first.
- As in the Middle Ages the image of a goat was latterly symbolic of the Devil but for centuries before that was a symbol of damnation. This suggests that neither Abraham Laverton nor John Taylor (the engraver of the Chandos portrait) thought highly of Shakespeare.
- The artist of the Chandos portrait (John Taylor) must have had directions to do what he did to the image of Shakespeare or he would have risked the wrath of people in high places.
- Whether or not Shakespeare knew of the damnation symbol is academic because he was by then caught between a rock and a hard place. If he was not the author of all the works attributed to his name his complaining might have resulted in a backlash. He might have felt a charlatan and thought it safer to stay quiet. He at least would not be around to have to endure it.

The evidence does not end there. What are supposed to be leaves in the first column of the window are also symbols of goats' heads. Above and below the image of Shakespeare thinly disguised brown and dark blue leafs 'point' towards his head and it appears that they are regarding it as a target. These images are crude birds-eye profiles of goats heads but fit the source of early Hebrew lettering that the designers of this window were clearly aware of as classicists.

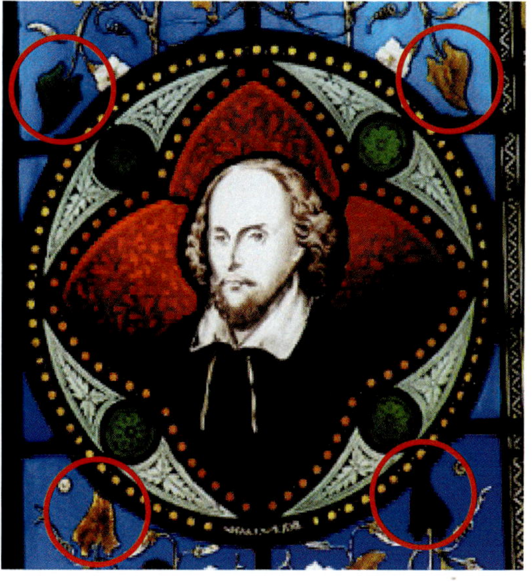

Red circles surround symbolic heads of goats regarding Shakespeare.

Behind each head are horizontal symbols of ears and behind those are horns.

'Tav' is translated as the Greek Omega whilst Alpha derives from pictorial script used in very early Hebrew texts. The lettering is found in contemporary Phoenician, Aramaic, Syriac and Arabic lexicons. Through time the lettering has morphed to become the letter 'T' in Greek, Latin and the significance of the letter Tav is that it is the last one in the word 'truth' and is held in classical Hebrew learning to be the counter-force to falsehood and deceit that Shakespeare is being tarred with here. The derivation of the letter is more important than what it spells out.

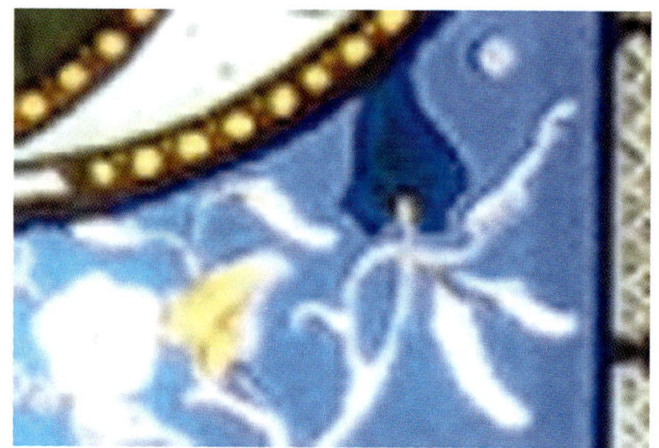

It must continue to be emphasised that these are symbols of goats and would never have been intended to look like your local Billy the Kid.

Here (right) is a bird's-eye view.

A further example demonstrates the full symbolism of the goat in what is drawn as a vine-like plant. It should be noted that this is a product of mid-Victorian England.

The image of William Shakespeare is one of the most famous in the world immortalised for many young baby boomer boy philatelists like myself by the 1964 face of a commemoration generation; a homely, slightly overweight, balding, could be anybody's uncle kind of guy from an engraving by Martin Droeshout in 1823.

Finding in due course he was not the real Shakespeare was extremely disappointing as this iconic figure became as famous in Shanghai as he was in Sheffield, as celebrated in Delhi as he was in Dover, as much read in Moscow as he was in Much Wenlock but looked nothing like the accredited favourites', shy-guy from '64.

Worse, the shady-looking guy supposed by the 'experts' to be the correct Shakespeare hosts a goat in his form and substance.

With a certain level of confidence from carrying out the above tests on the face that is among the National Portrait Gallery's finest I decided there was enough evidence that the Chandos portrait held concealed imagery to justify approaching the Gallery and asking them what they thought.

I really need not have bothered because an institution like the NPG operates as part of an establishment that listens only to 'experts'. Despite the art world having a history of gaffs second to none it is still the expert who carries the comfort blanket that provides succour when awkward issues arise.

Politely, charmingly but uncompromisingly I was dismissed out of hand.

However the curator I spoke to did continue to listen to my case and after around 30 minutes on the phone seemed to be reasoning my evidence. At one time the curator briefly left the phone for around 1 to 2 minutes and on return asked me 'Why would anyone do this to poor Shakespeare?' The significance of that question is open to a bit of speculation but it may simply have been a throw away comment.

At present some of the evidence forwarded has been retained by the Gallery's archivists but the curator has made it clear that no matter what I turned up it would not be looked into. Apart from the tightness of the Gallery's finances it held a review on this study area only in 2006 and have no plans to revisit this topic. To call this a disappointment is an understatement.

There are two basic reasons why it would be reasonable for the NPG to take some modest action with David Lawrence (on behalf of WTC) and myself. With the 400th anniversary of Shakespeare's death in the year 2016 it mayl be unethical for the NPG to fail to acknowledge to its visitors that there may be a concealed image in the portrait. Interestingly the NPG requested to know where the Laverton Stained Glass could be found and I told them exactly. As David Lawrence and I have already resolved much of what the Window is about and it is highly contextual it would seem logical that the NPG should rather ask what names they might keep as reference sources not where it is.

Secondly, the Westbury image of Shakespeare has in this book alone been demonstrated to have national importance. The Window warrants recognition for its remarkable and irreplaceable qualities that have been overlooked for 140 years.

The imagery here is far from the complete story of what Abraham Laverton and probably William Jervis Stent were getting at in their design of the first column of stained glass. There is the content of the cartouche at the top of the column that has strange qualities thoug. It is ostensibly the Abraham Laverton's coat of arms or family crest but why is it surrounded by sprites appearing to gesture towards it with the outline of two faces looking on? I do not know.

In any written reference to the Window there is always note of the two mottoes in the cartouches. In fact there are four. The third that has been missed was recorded for the first time by David Lawrence who spied it low down beneath the Laverton crest. In Latin it says *Basis Vertutum Constantia*. For all intents it appears to be positioned not to be seen. It translates as *The basis of virtue is constancy*. It is maybe better worded as *The foundation of virtue is steadfastness*. The fourth is discussed later in this section.

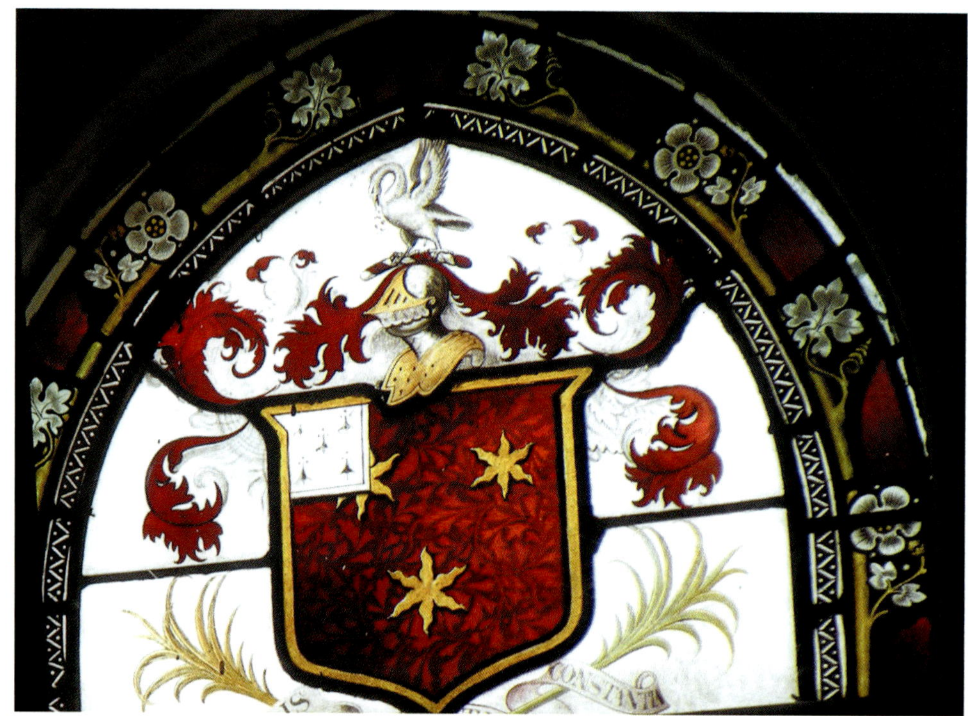

This is the typical view of the Laverton crest with the motto virtually hidden. The full content of this part of the window will be dealt with in Chapter 8 of this book.

Within the first column of the Stained Glass Window is observed to be an elaborate twisting and circling pattern of vines that in the Shakespeare panes are meant to look like they host the leaves and flowers adjacent to them. Careful attention reveals that the other three men have similar vines but not the same. The vine pattern in the window columns of No's 2, 3 and 4 look fairly certain to be what is termed the 'Freemason's vine.' The Shakespeare vine is different and not the Freemason's vine. Maybe this is Laverton's way of stating to those who have contended since Shakespeare died that he had been a Freemason that they got it wrong.

At this stage in the analysis of the content of the window something that cannot be ignored is whether or not Shakespeare deserves to be damned in this fashion. The question as to the authorship of his claimed literary works was not particularly doubted for more than 200 years after his death and the first well-known personage to raise the question, Ralph Waldo Emerson, did so in a relatively low key way.

Over the following ten years three characters came out of the closet of the Bard's detractors and published their doubts that Shakespeare had, or could have had, the talent to have written all that he had been credited for. These were Joseph C. Hart, Robert W. Jameson and Delia Bacon.

The main theory regarding the authorship suggests it was Francis Bacon, a celebrated essayist of the time with the ability and inclination to write such works of literature but also with reluctance to do so because of his political ambitions. The philosopher and scientist in the man further discouraged him from what was seen at the time as low level creativity. On the other hand he fraternised with the likes of Walter Raleigh and Ben Jonson who were devotees of street drama and are believed by the anti-Shakespeare lobby to have contributed in writing and transcribing texts themselves.

By the 1860s the country was overflowing with speculation and the authorship was one of the great issues of the time. Mock trials were played out in Britain and America, hundreds of books were published on the matter, secret ciphers and codes were offered up to supposedly interpret letters that both Bacon an Shakespeare sent each other. Fanciful ideas led to fanciful searches of unlikely places where Chinese whispers were supposed to originate and revelations of cryptic interpretations were promised.

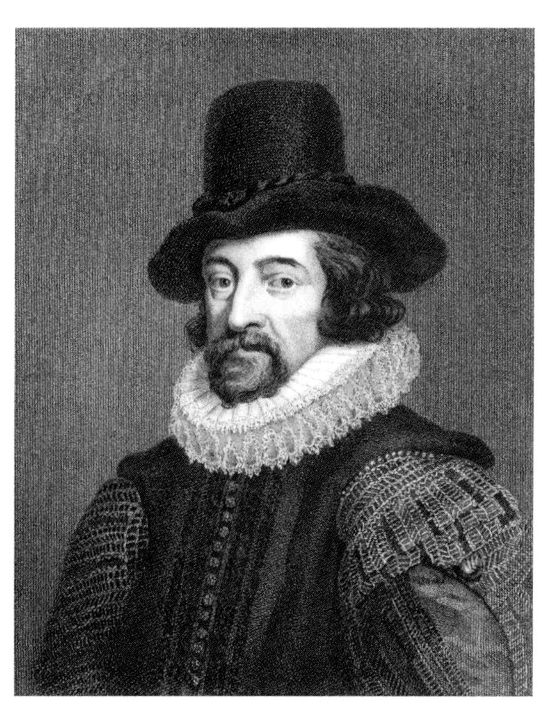

Engraving of Sir Francis Bacon.

Unsurprisingly they all came to nothing. Since the peak, frenzied years of Bard mania Bacon's role has faded in its popularity. In spite of the likes of Mark Twain favouring the Bacon authorship by the early 20th Century the most likely shadow writer was seen as being Edward de Vere, 17th Earl of Oxford, before attentions turned to Christopher Marlowe (poet and writer) and the 6th Earl of Derby. None has endured in the corporate mind of Shakespeare's readership. Over the hundreds of years since Shakespeare died there has been 'found' a plethora of information undermining who Shakespeare was and what he did, such as the discovery of the plays, Richard II, and, Richard III.

No matter to what extent these alternative authors have intruded into Shakespeare's time he remains the People's Bard. This makes it doubly hard today to write anything less than flattering about him. Considering that in his time he is recorded more than once fielding insults about his ' mimicry' Shakespeare is to be admired.

There is much more in the first main panel in column 1. For example the stained glass contains pictorial ciphers produced in similar fashion to those noted in column 3. The constellation and its asterism hidden this time is that of Orion, one of the most fascinating, romantic and awesome features of the winter night sky in the northern hemisphere. The significance of this asterism is that along with the Pleiades and Ursa Major it is one of only three formations of stars and galaxies mentioned in the Bible.

No other obvious issues exclusively arise out of a survey of column 1 of the window but three major functions of all four of the columns remain to be considered: solar eclipses, lunar eclipses and the content of respective cartouches or coats of arms/ family crests. The inclusion at the end of this chapter of an image of column 1 of the window is to maybe give some clue as to how for 140 years all this has been missed. Number one reason is simply that Abraham Laverton included much of the concealed imagery upside down. It is a ridiculously easy tactic but obviously a very effective one.

The way around it is to look at the image in the highly polished floor but again the focal lengths involved in doing so are elusive and everyone's instinct is to look up. For most functions the room would be decked with furniture. Protective plastic shields take away much of the clarity of what is to be seen and high up where much of the controversial stuff is to be seen the detail is fine.

Most people no longer have the skills sets to readily understand the astronomical, astrological, alchemical or factual knowledge of history and religion needed. For some of the higher order mathematical concepts our sound bite world makes few demands upon any of us for sustained spells of concentration or reiteration. It is of small wonder that so many of us seem to suffer from pathological myopia.

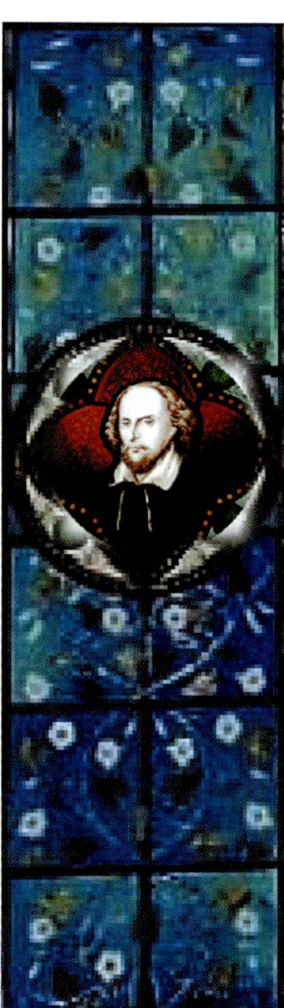

The images (left) are revisited to highlight a number of the features referred to above and followng:
- *Shakespeare's face and the symbolic goat,*
- *The solar prominences in red,*
- *Lines of suns around the prominences,*
- *The symbolic goat's head leaves,*
- *The asterism of Orion in the form of white flowers,*
- *Orion's belt and its reflection,*
- *The 'tav' shapes.*

Chapter 5

Isaac Newton, one of the cleverest men that ever lived.

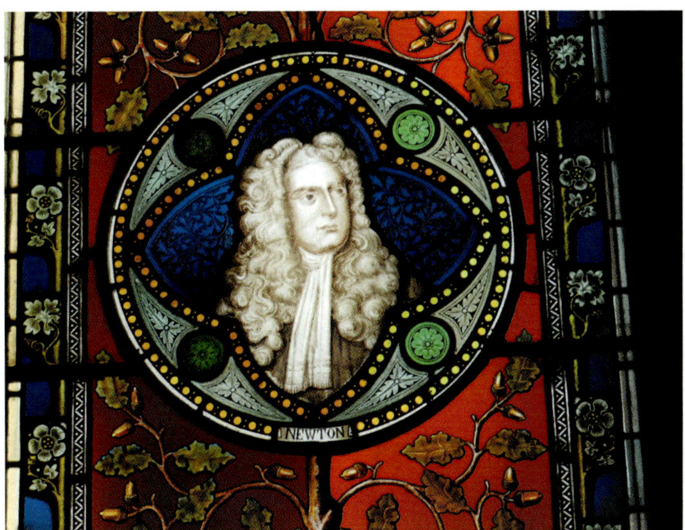

For the erudition of those who have lived their lives in a bubble Isaac Newton was unquestionably one of the greatest men who ever lived. If it turns out here that Abraham Laverton had just cause to impugn his character or professional standing as a mathematician or physicist it would be sensational indeed for all concerned.

'One of the cleverest men that ever lived' might be a bold statement about many a man but Newton set rules about gravity and motion, invented the reflecting telescope, formulated an empirical law of cooling, made groundbreaking studies about the speed of sound, 'invented' calculus, generalised the binomial theorem to non-integer exponents, was President of the Royal Society and allegedly survived an apple falling on his head.

Newton was no ordinary man but like many academic eccentrics he was inclined to make some bad decisions. The accusations of plagiarism that he made against his continental rival Leibniz in their common pursuit of infinitesimal calculus inspired hatred from not least members of his own University who long remembered him from his student days as a man with a chip on his shoulder.

Newton alienated other groups too including the Catholic Church and women, suggesting that he did not do things by halves but why would Abraham Laverton pick up on any of those issues for his condemnation?

There were two follies that might be considered as the major failings of a great eccentric. The first was the infamous South Sea Bubble. This was a scandal in the year 1720 when a British joint-stock company trading in public-private partnership for nearly ten years collapsed, ruining many of its investors even though its 'profitable wing', the slave trade, had been almost impossible to lose money on. Newton had got his fingers burned in a fiasco that embraced one of Laverton's pet hates, slavery.

If this was not reason enough maybe there was something more profoundly personal behind his being targeted by Laverton. As noted previously Laverton was more than a little interested in the practice of Alchemy and what it had to offer in terms of unbounded wealth and everlasting life. Newton had incidentally denied the Holy Trinity and the divinity of Jesus and neither of these two statements were statements that opened doors. Equally both Newton was at that time seeking support from any and every source. Newton had not pulled any punches in his appraisal of the Catholic Church as 'a harlot who had corrupted Christianity with non-biblical teaching.' A case of the kettle calling the teapot black when it is considered that Newton was driven by his quest to discover 'God's secret', uncover sacred writings, and expose those biblical writings that held in code so-called mythical truths.

In the late 19th century this would not have been a comfortable area for Abraham Laverton to pass judgement upon and maybe having set out to be critical of Newton he retreated back into himself in spite of an inate willingness to try to embrace new ideas.

Laverton trod lightly on the memory of Newton and of the four characters who appear in the Window the background of vines with oak leaves bearing acorns is a mix of symbols representing nationalistic loyalty, honour and various other virtues.

Did Laverton see Newton as a good man or were they bound together as Rosicrucians in common pursuit of the Philosopher's Stone that was and is the goal of that occult brotherhood? The stained glass window contains data paths associated with the prediction of solar eclipses that each man studied. As Laverton noted the head of each man is positioned as would be the Earth's moon in the occurrence of such an event but also clearly regarded this as a negative factor as light would be obstructed.

Newton openly revealed his occult commitments and boldly revealed his mathematical calculations that the world will end in 2060. Such too was the status of the man that along with others of his respected kind the government actually feared that, should practising alchemists discover the secret of changing base metals to gold, then the country's gold reserves could plummet in value, destabilising the nation.

The most difficult thing about each man's association with a secretive group or brotherhood is that they are secretive. Many books or other texts boast to tell of secret organisations or places, or rituals and so on but if the information is, say, in a book then where is the secret? After Newton's death he was found to have a phenomenal library of texts on Alchemy that together with his membership of the Royal Society that was a sort of Rosicrucian old boys' club saw him well and truly labelled as a disciple of the Rosy Cross.

Is it fair to tar Abraham Laverton with the same brush? It must be fair on at least one ground that being the frequency that the pelican bird occurs in the context of the Laverton Institute building and the town of Westbury as a whole. The pelican as the 'pelican in her piety' is a popular Rosicrucian scene that traditionally has the Mother Bird pecking at her own breast to draw blood to feed her starving chicks, something that is seen as symbolic of Christ on the Cross shedding His blood to save mankind.

This interpretation came late to the image of the Pelican, the story having been around since an early work titled the *Physologus* was produced in Alexandria in the 2nd century AD (CA) by three saints named Epiphianus, Basil and Peter. It became popular again in the Middle Ages as an allegorical resource about the legends of animal species and the Pelican story was found ready-made as a moral lesson in charitable giving. In 1321 Dante referred to it in his 'Divine Comedy', John Lyly mentioned it in 1606 in *'Euphues (the Anatomy of Wit)'* and Shakespeare wrote of *'the life-rendering Pelican'* in Hamlet in 1616.

The pelican is interchangeable with the Phoenix or the Swan and the latter is one of the five steps that has to be covered for Rosicrucians to achieve immortality. Laverton made no secret of how important he saw this and in the header of the first column of the Window his coat of arms contains this image, or so it is believed.

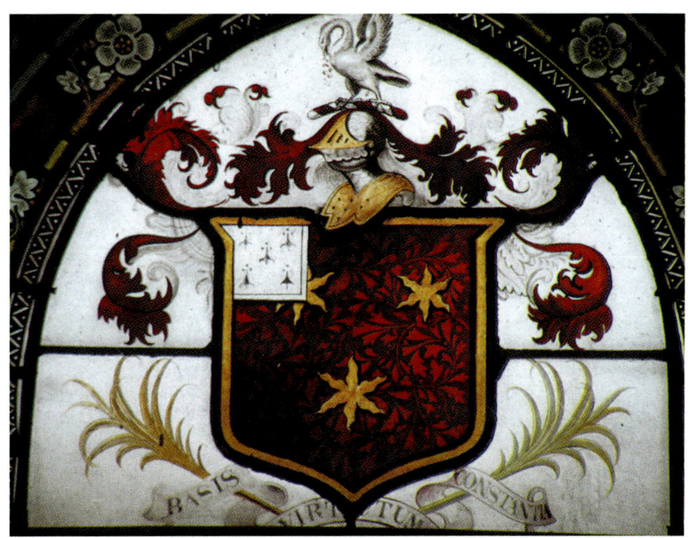

Abraham Laverton's personal coat of arms.

In the photograph of the coat of arms above there are no chicks and from the swan's beak there appears to be blood emanating. Equally confusing is the sculptured relief of a pelican in the stonework at the front of the Laverton Institute building. It is certainly not demonstrating exaggerated kindness (or piety) but appears in heraldic terms to be rampant. As if that is not confusing enough there is a stained glass image of Abraham Laverton himself in the north wall of All Saints Parish Church in which a distressed bird flounders amongst much blood for no apparent purpose.

What Laverton was getting at here is ambiguous. Is he declaring his faith in the brotherhood or is he mocking it? Equally there is a wealth of evidence that he was deeply committed to his Christian faith but could not resist embellishing his own image or that of his coat of arms with imps and sprites suggesting that he was also a joker and somewhat off the wall.

Maybe it is not worth pursuing the issue because this area of the Window on closer inspection is unfinished. Outlines may be seen when zooming in to finer detail of parts of the design that were never finished. Whether these areas were abandoned or time ran out in the execution of the task is unknown.

Whatever is the case the pelican is a symbol of the love of the creator for all mankind. Whether Laverton's mystic Christianity was founded in his occult Rosicrucianism and its associated Hermetic symbolism or not, nobody has understood his messaging for the past 140 years and during those five generations or more the world has radically changed.

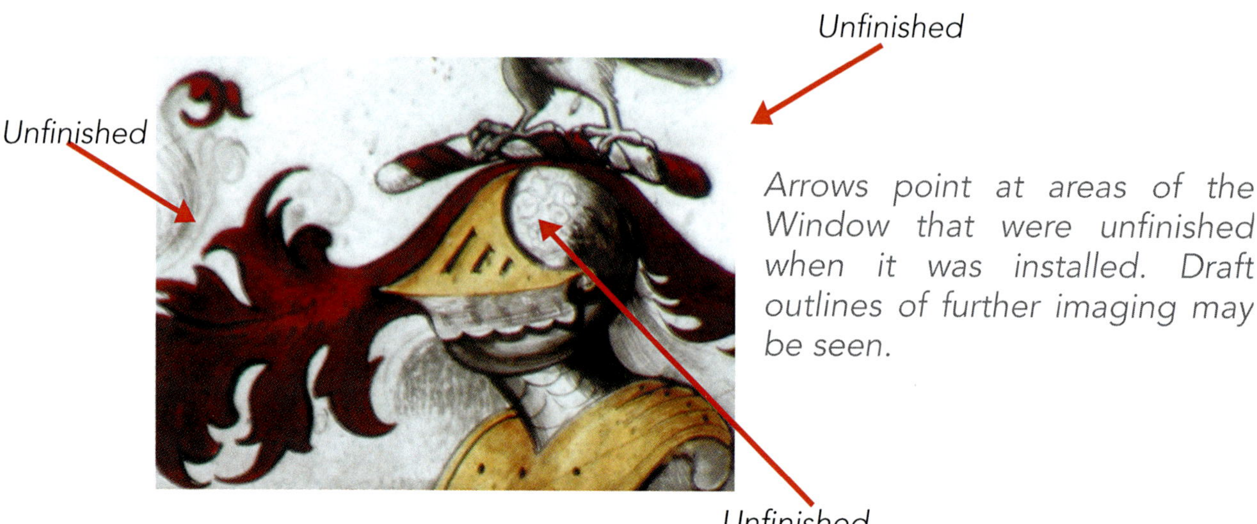

Arrows point at areas of the Window that were unfinished when it was installed. Draft outlines of further imaging may be seen.

Whatever the case the pelican is a symbol of the love of the Creator for all mankind. Whether Laverton's mystic Christianity was founded in his occult Rosicrucianism and its associated Hermetic symbolism, or not, nobody has understood his messaging for the past 140 years. During those five generations or more the world has radically changed.

The evidence of Laverton's Rosicrucian beliefs are substantiated by the content of the Window's asterisms and Newton would have been on the same wavelength in appreciating them. It is expressed in the Scottish rites of Alchemical Symbols for example that Ursa Major and its seven stars have profound alchemistic meanings with their indicative circling of the North Star that is supposedly linked to the chi or life force of the world.

Conceptually this may not be everyone's cup of theosophic tea but Rosicrucianism is like a box of pick and mix chocolates in that there is something for nearly everyone and one takes from it what one enjoys most. Its Alchemy divides the worlds of the divine, the human and the elemental and for reasons that will become apparent later. Laverton saw in the example of Newton the esoteric significance of his mathematics that could take him to a higher intellectual plane. Nowhere is that more manifest than in the Function Room of the Laverton Institute building today. It has held remarkable secrets for too long and it is time they were revealed.

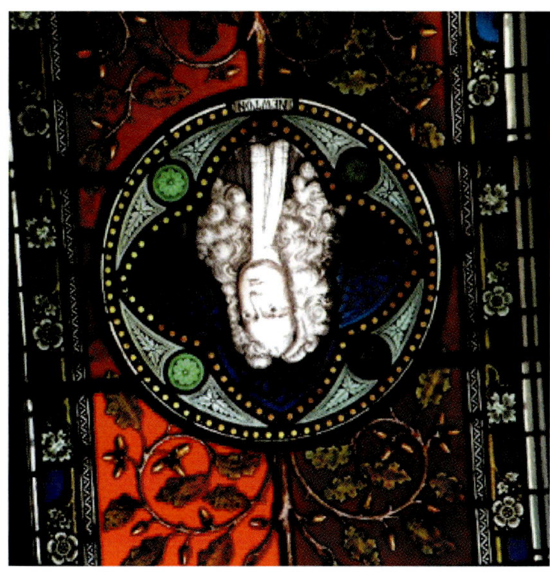

An inverted image of Isaac Newton

Although it is mentioned only fleetingly in this section so far the background constellation that Laverton associates with Newton is that of Andromeda. At the outset of researching this book it was far from obvious when we looked at astronomy and the asterisms of the Window just what the Newtonian distribution represents. The inclusion of such an intensity of symbols in the form mainly of acorns hinted at a feature like the Milky Way.

On the other hand the header at the top of the column that shows an industrial scene was a big distraction as it appears to have little to do with Newton or the time in which he lived. As is noted at the start of Chapter 9 following, Newton was a genius but his life was also one full of distractions and for each of his great achievements there was seemingly an inevitable downside that in combination meant that Laverton could be placing him in the Window for any one of a myriad of reasons.

For example, his most productive period of devising new mathematical methods and formulae coincided with his retreat to Lincolnshire when the Great Plague was at its peak between 1665 and 1667. He had a long running feud with his rival Leibniz in the independent developments of differential calculus but ultimately won the day. Would Laverton have seen this positively or negatively; or a case of nationalism versus internationalism?

Laverton would have definitely been supportive to each man as a final say. He may not have won the world over to his way of thinking but when the data analysis played out he was probably more of a winner than a loser.

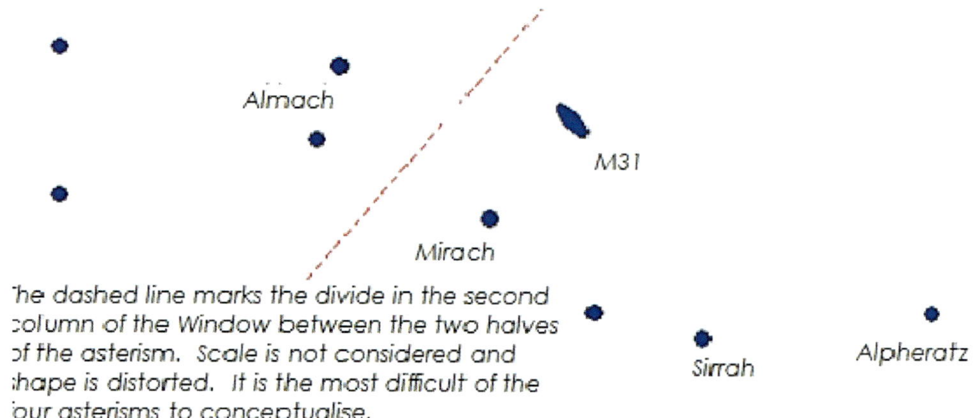

The dashed line marks the divide in the second column of the Window between the two halves of the asterism. Scale is not considered and shape is distorted. It is the most difficult of the four asterisms to conceptualise.

It is impossible to know what Abraham Laverton was thinking when he created such elaborate backdrops to the four columns of the Westbury Window. Why did he create such starry designs when constellations lend themselves so poorly to the task? Why did he choose such obvious asterisms without any notable moral or lesson to be taught or learned from them? Why try and disguise them if the point was to moralise anyhow?

Contradictions abound and all answers to these kind of questions are speculative. Given that the constellations are dressed as vegetation of one kind or another, do any of those plants have pertinent characteristics? It was mentioned earlier what the traditional meaning of the acorn was so could there be any other significant symbolism.

Below is an example of Newton's genius, the Newton cradle used to demonstrate some fundamental principles of mass, force and gravity through the transfer of momentum and energy. This kind of creative application is what we associate with Newton today.

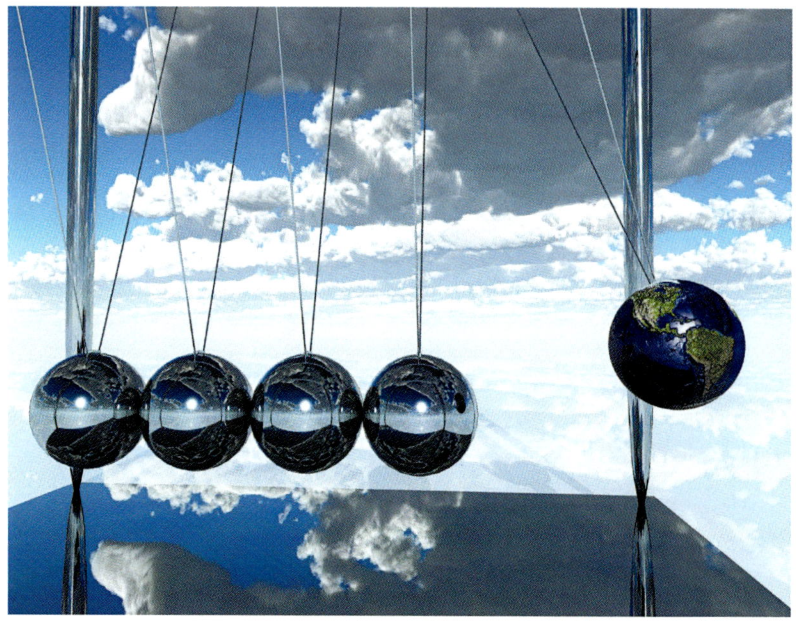

Newton's Cradle

Chapter 6
James Watt, a great Briton?

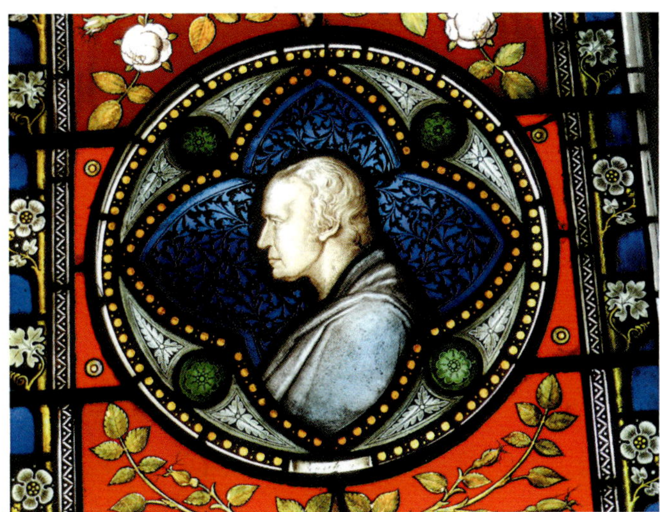

The easiest panel to 'read' if the viewer has the requisite skills sets is Unit 3, that being the unit housing the likeness of James Watt. Using the *Sketch diagram for identifying main panels in stained glass units* it is possible to navigate the window and reasonably closely refer to any feature.

Of those who have viewed this window there appears to have been nobody who has recorded the fact that each head is positioned as that of the Moon in the event of a total solar eclipse. The margins of each inset or cartouche (a word here used in a cartographic manner of referral as to a map excerpt) are studded with hundreds of 'suns' as are the margins of the bulbous prominences surrounding them. The shapes of these prominences are reminiscent of recorded imagery of the Pembrokeshire eclipse of 8th April 1652 and another observed in Cambridge on 3rd May 1715.

Intriguingly around each of the heads are four spheres. A major part of the key to understanding the Window lies in its representations of parts of the solar system, our galaxy and the universe. Interestingly there are only three constellations of stars in the night sky mentioned in the Bible and each is found represented in the imagery of this window. These are the asterisms of Orion, Ursa Major and the Pleiades. Hiding them in the big picture must have given the creators of the Window great amusement and arguably they did too good a job as it has taken a long time for somebody to see them.

The Unit of stained glass that is most easy to understand is the third from the left with James Watt at its centre. Like the other three it has the decorative character of an Egyptian sarcophagus dating from more than 1300 B.C., but anyone might surely question the stand-out quality of the white rose-like flowers? Apparently not.

When the distribution of those flowers is plotted separately as shown in Part b) of the diagram for Unit 3 things are not much clearer. However if the left and right halves of the unit are regarded as reflections of each other something very obvious appears as shown in Unit 3, Parts c and d of the diagram, namely the asterism of the Plough or Big Dipper from the constellation of Ursa Major otherwise known as the Great Bear.

Having got this far when I first considered the window there was clearly the approximate shape of the asterism of Ursa Major but it was not accurate with regard to one star.

This is an important lesson as it informs the reader of the Window that for all the genius behind it the integrity of some clues has been compromised by the need to make some distributions topological and in this instance it is done by ignoring linear scale. The correct flower substituted produces the very obvious inclusion of the star Megrez and the following pattern for which it was intended.

Unit 3, Parts a) & b)

Unit 3, Part b

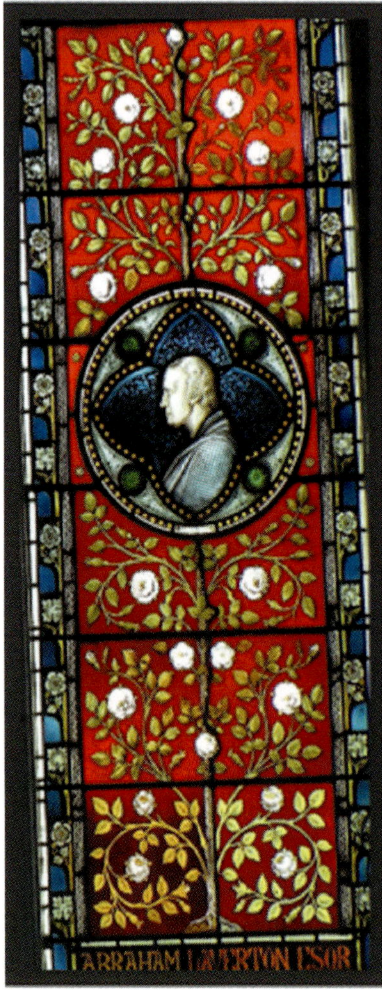

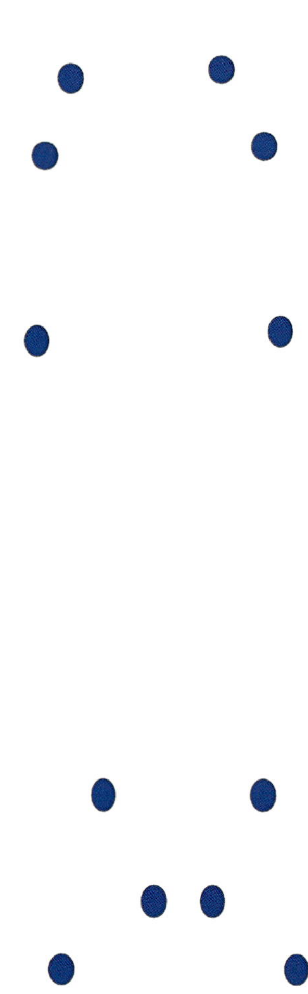

Unit 3, Part c & d

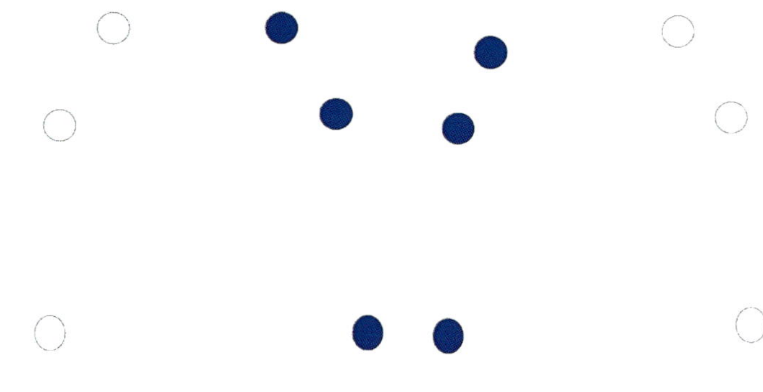

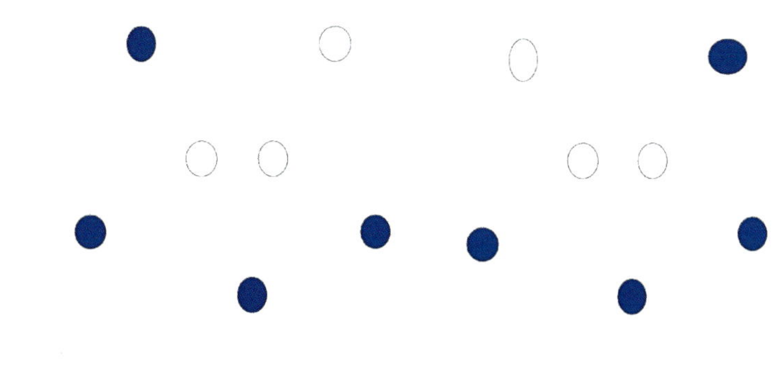

Unit 3, Part e

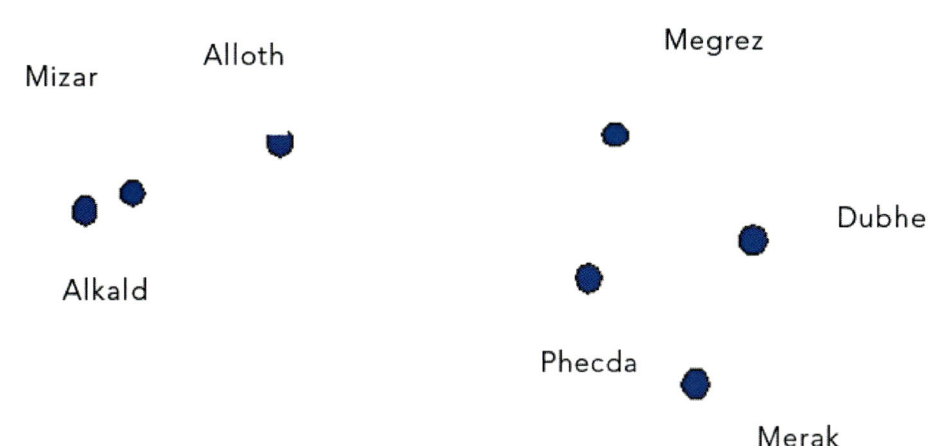

A number of issues already beg to be addressed and extrapolated in this part of the Window. The first of these is for what reason did James Watt incur the disdain of Abraham Laverton? Watt is seen today as one of the pantheon of British scientists who put the 'Great' in Britain. As an inventor and engineer he played a major role in the Industrial Revolution and has often been acclaimed too as one of the most important men that ever lived.

His main contribution was to improve the operational efficiency of the steam engine and hence make it financially realistic to use. It was not necessarily so and what is apparent is that it was only successful when he went into partnership with Matthew Boulton in 1775.

Watt went on to be a wealthy man as a result of the patent that Boulton took out for him in 1775 and again in 1800. It was Edward Bull who actually made the engines that Watt designed and unfortunately they ended up falling out, going to court to sue each other and, as is the way of the world, the only winners were the lawyers.

As time went by Watt became a national hero and Boulton was largely forgotten. This did not sit well with a lot of people and even more influential academics and entrepreneurs were irritated by Watt's role in the water controversy that kicked off in the 1780s.

Basically, Henry Cavendish discovered that water formed from two gases that he called inflammable air (hydrogen) and dephlogisticated air (oxygen) where it was previously thought to be an element along with fire earth and air. James Watt Jnr. claimed that his father had been the discoverer. The scientific community fell in behind one or the other and Watt commanded even more antipathy.

A third reason why Watt may have engendered bad feeling towards himself was the poor relationship he had with the brilliant Richard Trevithick, the man popularly believed to have invented the first high pressure steam locomotive. This was something that Watt thought to be impossibly dangerous but when Trevithick was promoted to chief engineer at the Ding Dong mine near Penzance in Cornwall he produced just such an engine and it revolutionised transport in the industrial parts of South West England and South Wales.

Anybody who cared to call himself a scientist at the time saw immediately the possibility of the development of a steam locomotive. In a short time Trevithick's high pressure steam locomotive was built and proved it could pull up to ten tons of iron at speeds of nearly five miles per hour for close to ten miles. However, James Watt continued to stigmatise Trevithick's invention and even stated that he deserved 'hanging' for having produced it. Trevithick became a broke and broken man failing to get backing for his inventions not least because Watt had refused to acknowledge his achieving something that he had failed to do himself.

The irony of all this is made acutely in the cartouche or inset at the head of Watt's column in the stained glass window. It is discussed in that chapter later in this book.

How much of Laverton's disenchantment with the like of Watt stemmed from his own fraternising with the big noises in the railway bonanza of the middle decades of the 19th Century is a footnote to this section. The sanctioning of railway companies was extremely controversial and even when they were set up they oozed bad blood between stockholders, directors and managers.

Often there was conflict between personal and family capital, an abandonment of any ethical business structure, a blurring of the boundaries between the interests of the railway companies and the big businesses they supported, too few controls on any of the main players and the preponderance of some pretty primitive accounting and auditing. Abraham Laverton witnessed this close up and must have felt that the worse injustices stemmed from Watt's day and his uncompromising obsession with self interest. Watt was not his kind of man. Herbert Spencer called it 'graspiness'.

Trying to guess what was in Abraham Laverton's mind is pointless. There were many parameters acting upon him not least when he donned his politician's hat. The overriding question left unanswered is why Ursa Major? There is symbolism everywhere suggesting that he may have been a Rosicrucian in which case the answer to the question will definitely never be known as the Rosicrucians were the most secretive of all the so-called occult, cabalistic, theosophic brotherhoods.

Most of the likely answers that any Rosicrucian association might suggest are to say the least ugly with more than a touch of the Hollywood 'B' movie about them. But there is one that I could give credence to and that is based on the perception that Ursa Major does not look like a bear, nor a plough, nor a big dipper. It does, or so the idea goes, look like a sheep fold and maybe there is an analogy with the 'good shepherd' embracing lost or wayward members of his flock. I would like to think so.

In this investigation there are plenty of side issues or matters of other interest that are too good to ignore. In this section one point of interest that is found relates to the image of James Watt that occurs in the Window. It is not a familiar likeness of Watt but is of superb quality.

The likeness is taken from a sculpture of Watt made by Francis Leggatt Chantrey who was born in Derbyshire in 1781. From a modest education he became a carver in 1802 but proved at that same time to have a considerable talent as a portrait painter. Combining his talents he became a modeller of busts and made a considerable impact with his very first commission.

By 1808 he was solely a sculptor and the following year he was commissioned to carve a bust of the King, George III. In 1810 he exhibited at the Royal Academy and that same year also sculpted William Pitt. The quality of his work is staggeringly good and there is a public walkway in the town of Westbury named after him (although it may also be named after an alter in the parish church of All Saints dedicated to the founder for whose soul endowments would have been raised. Evidence supporting either case is not substantial).

Chapter 7
Edwin Henry Landseer, a tragic genius

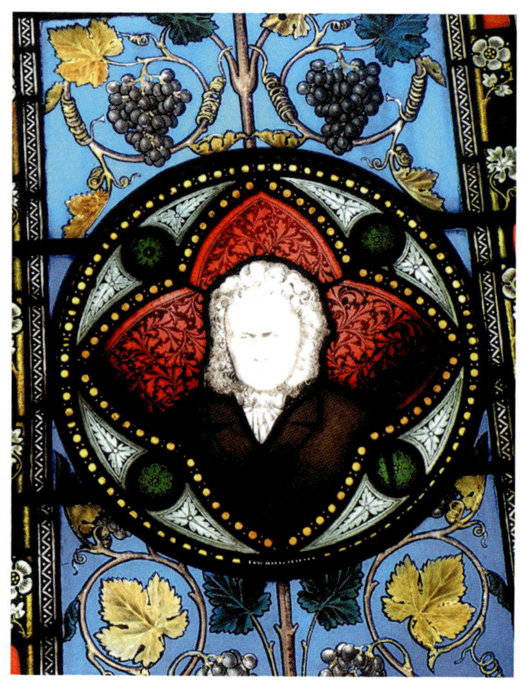

Edwin Henry Landseer was a great artist, a great sculptor, a great favourite of Queen Victoria and a national icon but his life was a classic story of a wayward genius haunted by his own demons that were manifest in weaknesses for alcohol and drugs and his moods of depression leading to insanity.

For most of the people most of the time history has been kind to Edwin Landseer. His paintings such as the Monarch of the Glen, his sculptures such as the lions at the foot of Nelson's column, even his annoyingly anthropomorphic rescue dogs arriving at some calamitous scenes each with their half gallon of finest malt whisky strapped under their chins were, painting after painting, beloved by all of the people some of the time.

Landseer even has a breed of Newfoundland dog named after him that is famed for its courage, gentleness, loyalty, intelligence and other virtues. In his art, particularly his paintings, virtues were symbolised in a naïve and candid way but the same could not be said of Landseer the man who surf-boarded the tidal wave of Victorian schmaltz whilst nefariously exploiting racial stereotypes, the xenophobia of the nation's addiction to the trappings of Empire and good, old fashioned bigotry.

Abraham Laverton saw one of the nation's favourites as a sinister influence who was to be reviled.

On literally face value alone the image of Landseer in the stained glass window has an obvious sinister quality about it. It is not the face of a friendly uncle or affectionate grandfather, more the mug-shot of some desperado off a wanted poster in a monochromatic Elstree who-done-it. What Abraham Laverton was getting at here was that he was bringing to the public awareness the very troubling, harmful bigotry that underlay much of Landseer's work.

It was suspected by many and known by a few that his prejudices ran deep in his work beyond the ridiculous content of his paintings such as where he had a man named van Amburgh relaxing in a large cage with a lion, a tiger, a cheetah, a leopard and sundry other wildlife (that would naturally tear each other apart) enjoying a siesta together without so much as the crack of a whip.

Unfortunately there was a recurring duality in his work that is clearly demonstrated where in his painting of 'Uncle Tom and his Wife for sale' two distinctly human dogs, the facial characteristics of which more than just resemble certain racial stereotypes. Elsewhere dog breeds painted by Landseer such as pugs were caricatures of all that was most obscene in one man's prejudice against the colour of another man's skin. An often quoted remark is that by the abolitionist John Brown regarding the 'amazing' racial stereotyping hits the nail on the head but is not justifiably quotable here. Some things do not need repeated.

The controversial content of Landseer's work was against a cultural malaise in Britain and its Empire that revolved around the Slave Trade. Popular opinion in the wider world was turning dramatically against the idea that one man could be another man's property. Abraham Laverton watched Landseer's perverse tweeness being used to sweeten the bitter taste of slavery and the subjugation of the black man in society. Laverton could not hold back his disgust and when the opportunity arose in this Window he lashed out at Landseer and the twisted values he espoused in his art.

In the twelve panes of the fourth and last main column of the Window the asterism of the Pleiades in the constellation of Taurus the Bull is used to structure an outing of Landseer's shameful bigotry. The reason for his choosing to use bunches of black grapes to represent star clusters of the constellation in general and the Pleiades in specific is a no brainer and I find it unbelievable that anyone with eyesight something close to 20:20 with or without spectacles can look at the graphic in the top left corner of the top right pane and not appreciate the irony that Laverton is using to condemn Landseer.

This graphic of leaves (many coloured yellow or dark brown) and grapes has only a shallow disguise of the contempt that they represent for Landseer's art. The 'faces' could hardly be more offensive.

The most cutting personal attack by Laverton on Landseer is one that the former man probably thought would never be exposed and he must have sat for years in his retirement smirking impishly (the way he was inclined to do) at so many people passing the Window by but never seeing the lambasting he was daily delivering to Landseer.

For if the Window is once more inverted there appears in Landseer's sideburns what he abused many times in his art and what he felt so wrongly repulsed by and superior to. Abraham Laverton turned the tables even though it has taken so long for somebody to spill the beans.

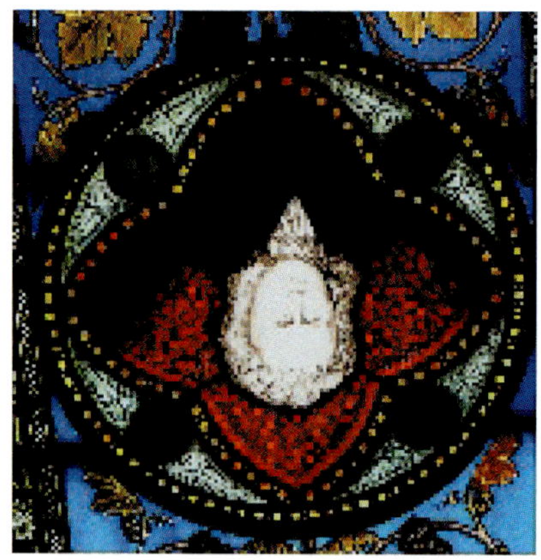

In the enlarged image below there appears to be a distinctive symbol of Freemasonry disguised in Landseer's neckpiece. Can you see it? There are also some unpleasant 'faces' concealed in his hair and sideburns. Can you see them? A brief scan of Landseer's own work mentioned above will help with seeing some ugly inclusions.

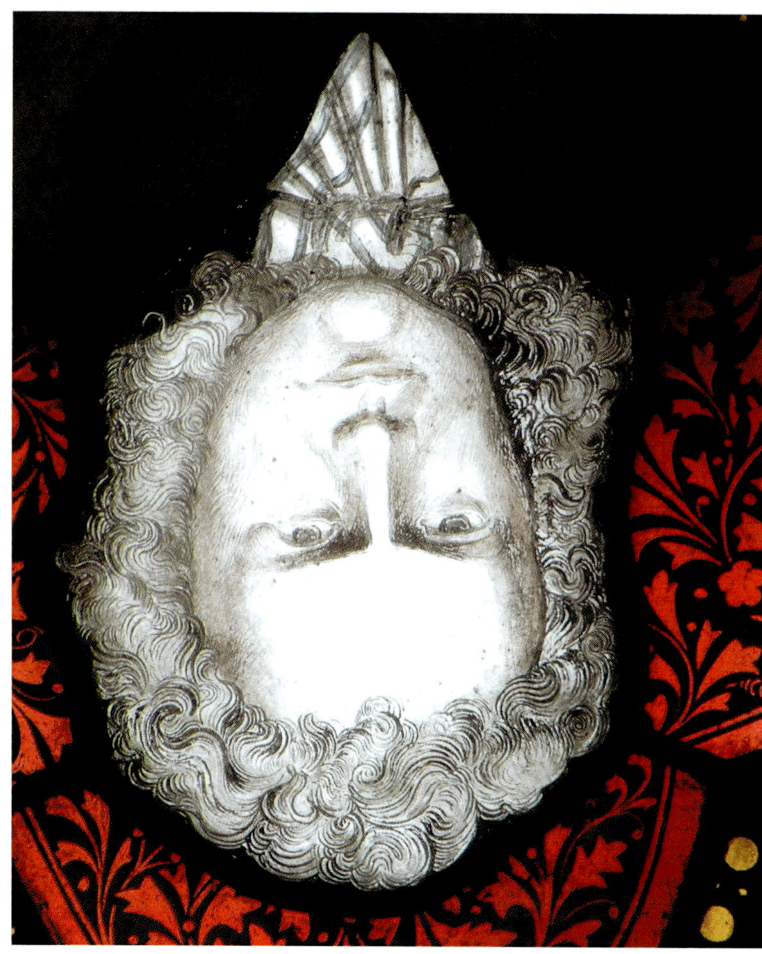

Regarding the graphic above, a tip for those who would ever do research of primary data sources, never use inferior equipment or work to less than the best standards because you may never know what you are missing. I took the photo and thought that maybe it was as good as it gets. I tried again and found of the two images one to be an aberration and the latter one a revelation.

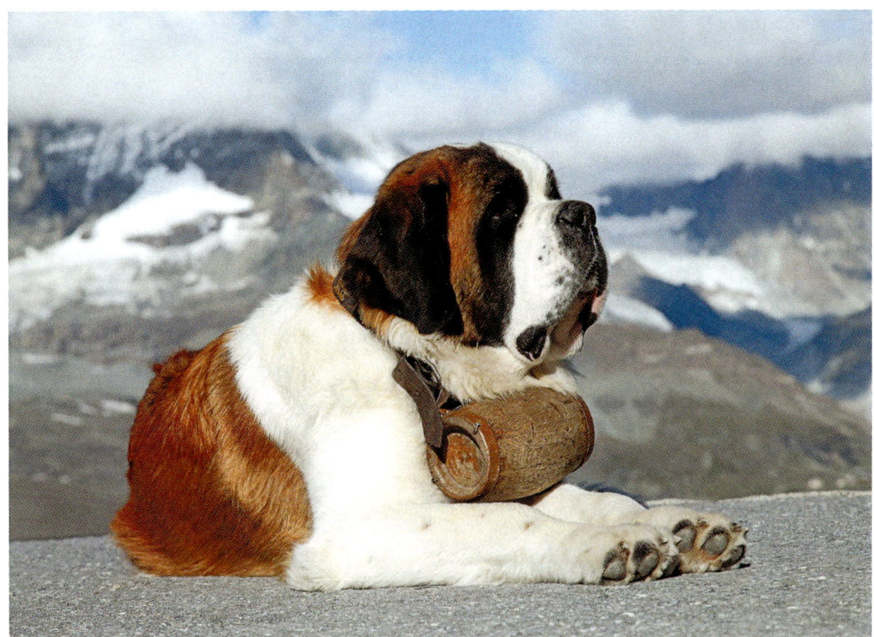

Image in the fashion of Landseer'sl mobile distillery.

The fresh image below does not reveal much either on initial inspection but as with all these elusive Victorian visual challenges perseverance invariably pays off. Laverton must have paid some skilled artists a handsome sum for such complex, devious, and clever work.

It is as though Laverton is striking back at Landseer in kind for his lifetime of indiscretions all of which cannot have helped his declared insanity the same year as the Window was installed, 1873 and his subsequent death.

For examples of the kind of tasteless anthropomorphism that a pragmatic man like Abraham Laverton may have been irritated by I refer the reader to works such as 'Laying down the law; trial by jury', painted in 1842, or 'Windsor Castle in Modern Times, 1840 - 1845.' As an insult to any average man's intelligence who is grounded by the realities of an industrial environment Landseer's 'Portrait of Mr van Amburgh' beggars belief. Just as offensive is his painting titled Diogenes and Alexander. There are plenty of others.

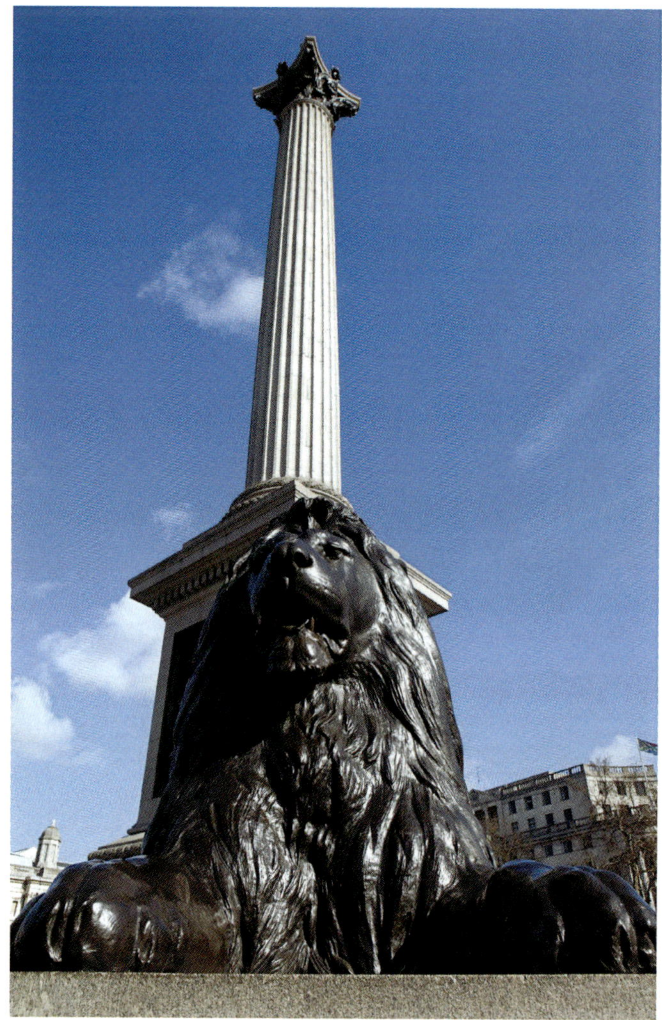

Lions at Trafalgar Square - sculpted by Landseer.

Conventional wisdom is now so prescriptive with regard to any issue that affronts political correctness one wonders how Landseer would have fared in 21st century Britain. Would he have settled into a niche market such as jigsaw design or chocolate box covers, or would he have rebelled to be associated with a Banksy or an Andy Warhol?

He does seem to have been an establishment man and served his time wearing dead men's shoes until the weeds in his garden blossomed into prize flowers and in his turn he was President-elect of the Royal Society. Showing an acute awareness of his own shortcomings he turned the position down.

Given that even his apologists labelled him 'crazy' and 'tortured' it must have been difficult for men like Laverton to watch Landseer attain such academic acknowledgement and popularity. Contemporaries though write of a man who was the life and soul of any party, excellent company, a natural performer, socially adroit, mixing easily between the monarch and the street beggar.

Abraham Laverton would not have reasoned Landseer's shortcomings whether he was ill or not. There was no excuse that Landseer could have come up with to mitigate some of his worst shortcomings.

Laverton was not alone in disliking Landseer and Prince Albert, husband of Queen Victoria, openly demonstrated his contempt for Landseer not only before his family but many times in public. He apparently did not like his art, his subject matter or the prices he charged. This caused tension in the royal household and eventually Landseer was squeezed out of the closer family circle much to his embarrassment.

Sadly Landseer died when relatively young and loved or hated he left an indelible impression on English society. His human failings were not unique and the Victorian world he lived in did him few favours.

Whether by spite, dislike, contempt or whatever the Laverton image of Edwin Landseer oozes revenge largely by way of ugly images concealed in his hair, sideburns and cravat.

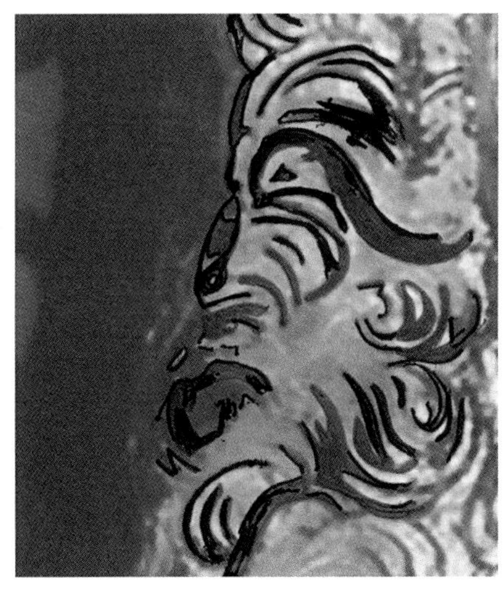

The most striking (not surprisingly for the creator of the Trafalgar Square lion sculptures) is what appears to be a close relative of the beast that followed Dorothy along the Yellow Brick Road.

Putting animal imagery into Landseer's most personal space is a kind of rough justice for those taken advantage of, mocked or humiliated by him.

All I have done here is trace over the composite detail of the face and paw of a lion that has clearly been painted as a mocking gesture.

Chapter 8

The Abraham Laverton Crest (Header Panel Number 1)

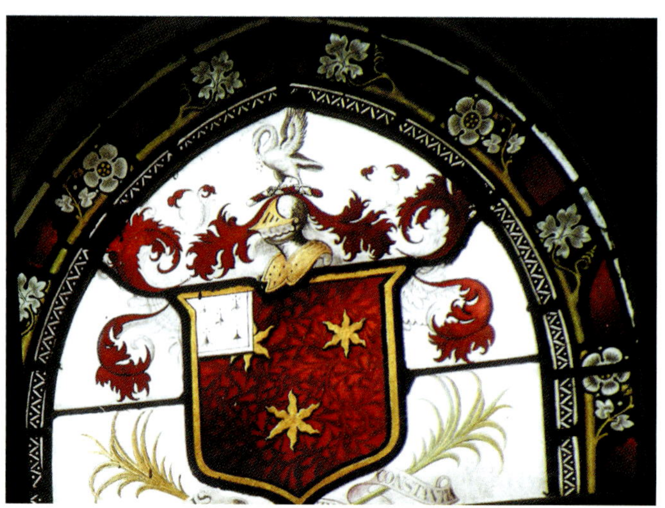

The contents of this header panel have been noted already but a little more thought throws up some anomalies worth attention. Any reference to it should be as the Crest of Abraham Laverton. It is not a family crest and as there is no record of this branch of that family fighting for their country it should not be regarded as a shield.

If the bird at the top of the panel is intended to be a pelican in its piety there should be chicks, seven of them. There are none so it is not the creature of charitable mythology. The strange white panel at the top left of the shield has five shapes on it similar to a playing card. These shapes have no easy to come by explanation but having three, clawed feet the closest fit answer to what they are places them in the darkest areas of possible reasoning.

The ugly, spooky sprites are a playful quirk of Laverton's alter ego, a side of the man that is not easily understood. All Saints Parish Church houses the smaller Laverton stained glass shown below. (The shield badge is found in both places.) The two other characters overseeing Abraham Laverton in prayer are hideous 'familiars' (imps) whose role is not apparent. There is much here that is yet to be resolved.

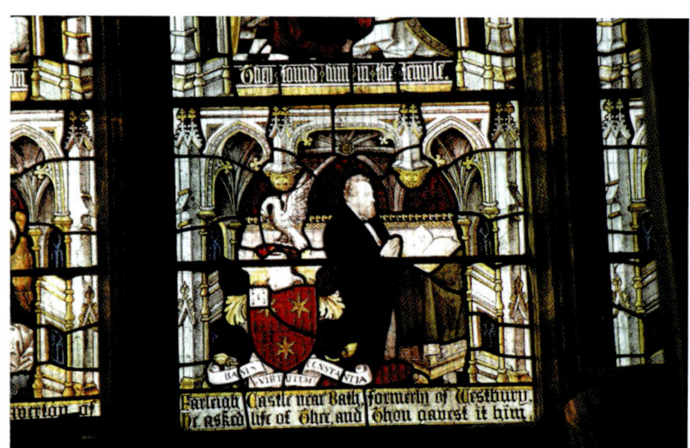

The window dedicated to Abraham Laverton in All Saints Church

Even with his journey to the Choir Invisible imminent Laverton could not resist including the hideous faces of imps shown in the backdrop.

b)   The Factory of the 19th Century (Header Panel Number 2)

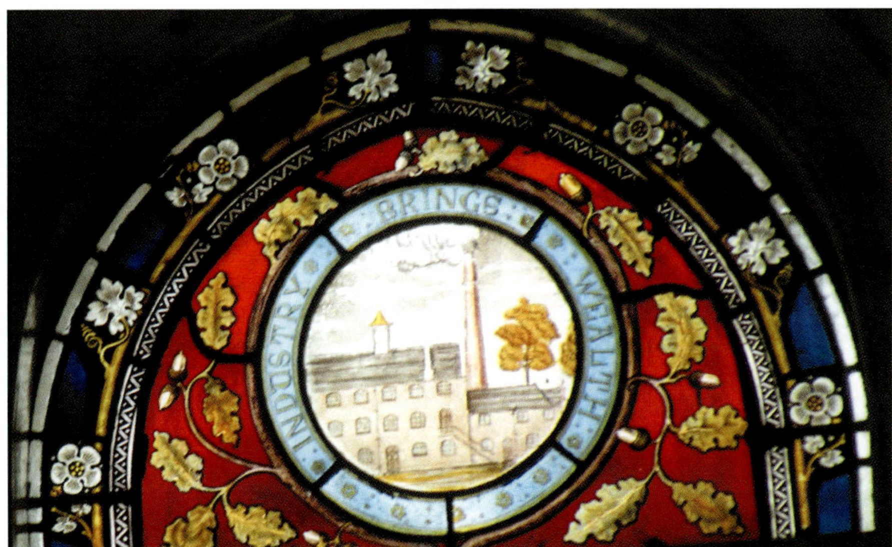

I have been asked many times why I have been the only person in 140 years to see through the Window and understand what it is about. The inference is always that if what I write about is correct then somebody will have seen it before. The further inference is that what I write in this book is 'my interpretation' and not a reality. It is my flight of fancy.

This header panel does a lot to blow that kind of thinking away. I find it impossible to believe that nobody has noticed even one of the concealed images/messages in this header panel over the years. Upside down, sideways or inside out surely one person should have seen something? Anything! It is the reporting, recording and collating of such observations that is missing.

Laverton employed his usual deceptive device of turning this artwork upside down. On this occasion his ploy was a huge success as the original meaningful scene becomes a radically different one when inverted. The key features are:

- An ostensibly ordinary factory,
- with ordinary windows for such a building,
- air pollution being emitted from a tall chimney stack,
- a fire escape on the outside of the factory,
- grilled windows,
- a motto, *"Industry brings wealth"*

It all ties together sensibly in Abraham Laverton's mid-Victorian world.

Look closer and nothing is what it seems.

The factory building is a disturbing structure with faces in most of the grilled windows. They look more like prisoners than factory employees and Laverton is making some sort of statement here. Chartists? Tolpuddle Martyrs? I do not know.

The zoomed images below make for an easier view of what is to be understood here.

Upright version

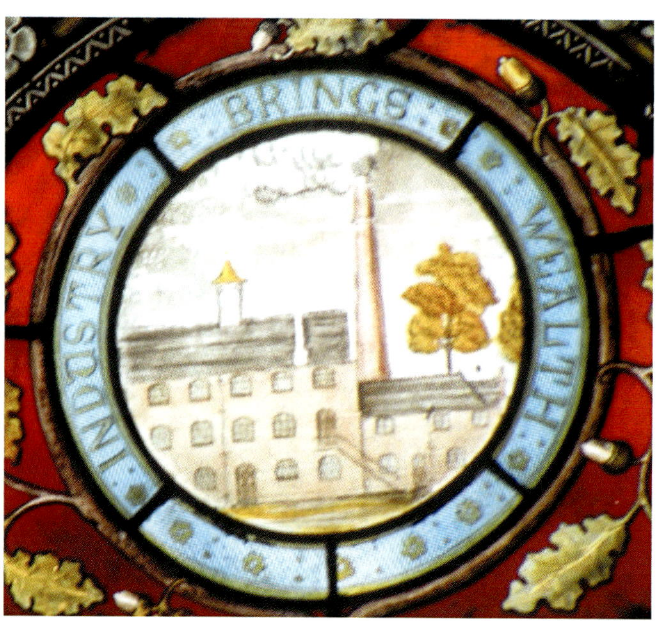

Inverted Version (Upside down)

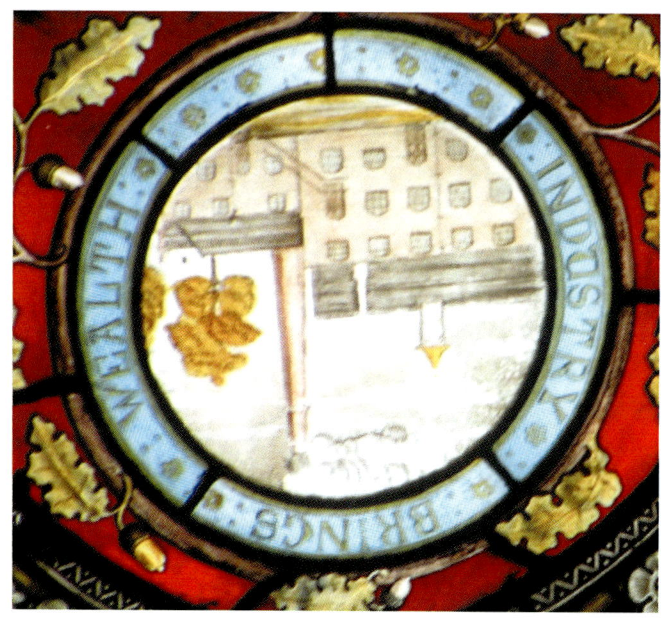

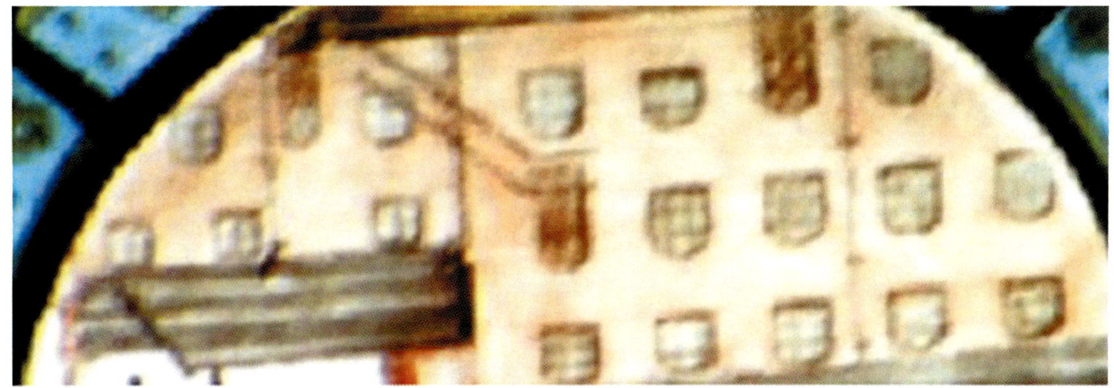

For the purposes of this publication the image is enlarged to show as much detail as possible without becoming hopelessly pixelated. Most every window in the factory has a face looking out of it. Some are very obvious like that in bottom right hand corner and some are more difficult to see. What is undeniable is that no two windows look the same. Why would anyone take such trouble?

By simply increasing contrast and darkening the image using standard PC software the faces emerge from their bright bleached hiding place. See diagram above.

The next thing to note is the 'factory chimney' from which steam or smoke is being emitted. Again with simple image manipulation it may be seen that there is a less than attractive face smoking the fumes. Who? Why? I do not know. (See below)

The clarity of the image is lost by trying to make it visible on paper but up front and personal it is quite disturbing.

This is no less weird than the next part of the image to be revealed; that is the golden coloured tree to the right of the Header.

Inverted it is not a tree but an ageing man and younger woman on what appears to be a carousel ride. There is a canopy over their heads and their fairground ride circles the chimney stack that has now become the spindle about which their ride rotates. (See next page)

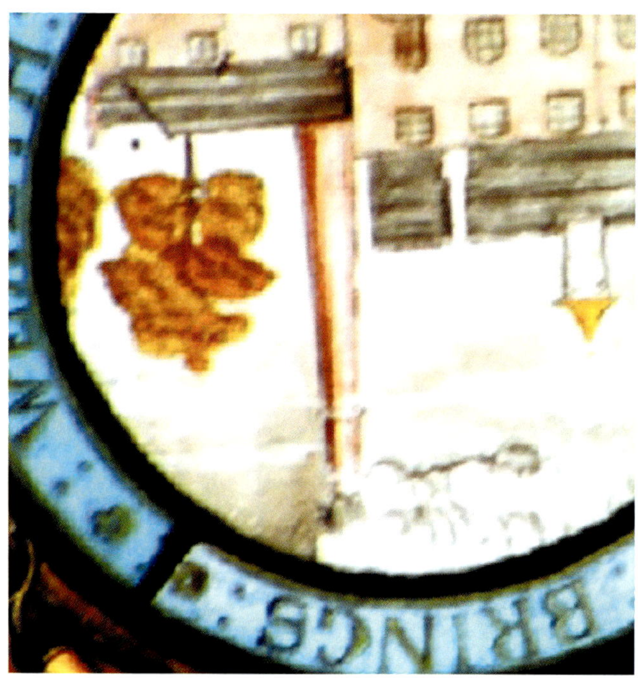

I have not presently got the vocabulary to accurately describe the structure of Victorian fairground rides.

In the Window itself the image of the woman's face is clear enough to find a photographic match for. Maybe we already have one.

The most surprising feature of this header is not in the picture but the significance of the legend that encircles the graphic. The words have important significance in the Islamic world as they come from the laws set out in The Holy Book of The Qur'an (39.63) that states:

> The reward for patience is success, the punishment for indolence is privation, industry brings wealth, steadfastness brings victory.

Just how this all fitted into the mind of Abraham Laverton is perplexing.

It is not well documented how in his early years in the woollen industry Abraham Laverton made enough money to go on and do all that he did but somewhere he picked up a very profound education in the classics, religion, technology and science as well as moral virtue, sound economics, social justice and political gamesmanship.

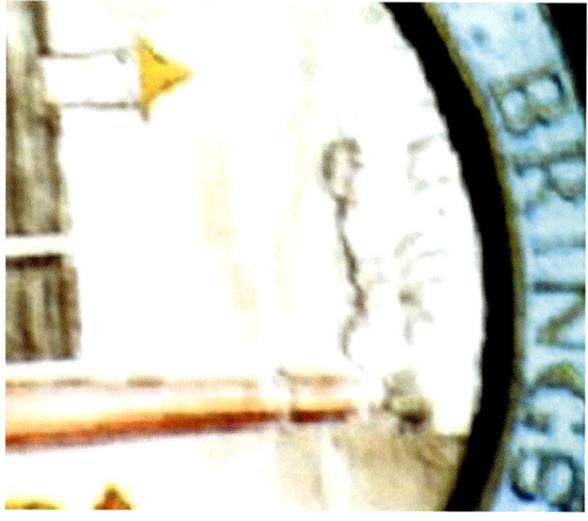

The greatest challenge for him was to live truly by the standards he set for others. In this header graphic his ethical values ooze out from the Window and pose a plethora of further questions.

It is likely these are details that have never been seen, appreciated or understood in the Window.

c)   'Watt's' Steam Locomotive (Header Panel Number 3)

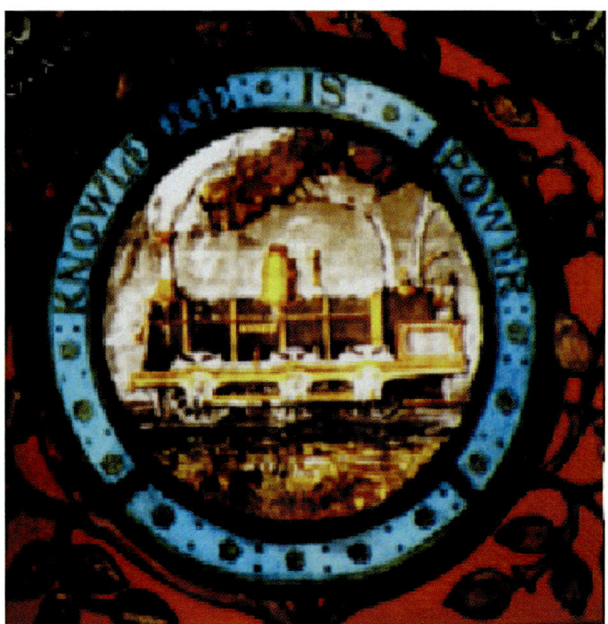

'Knowledge is Power'

This is the only case where the header matches the person about who the particular stained glass column is dedicated. As noted it is a graphic that mocks James Watt and does not praise him.

As mentioned earlier it was only in partnership with Matthew Boulton that Watt's steam engine became a production model. It was only with Edward Bull that a working model came off the design sheet and it was only after Richard Trevithick had produced a working locomotive that Watt took his ambition to its logical outcome sadly to the breaking of Trevithick's fragile spirit of endeavour and even more fragile financial backing.

For those who will open their eyes a little wider there is some extraordinary imagery in this panel. Challengingly, those with their eyes wide open will also have to balance upside down at the top of a 12 foot stepladder. It was a trick of Abraham Laverton to conceal many of his more poignant visual statements by displaying them upside down and he excels himself here.

Having achieved this precarious balancing act there are several curious things to behold.

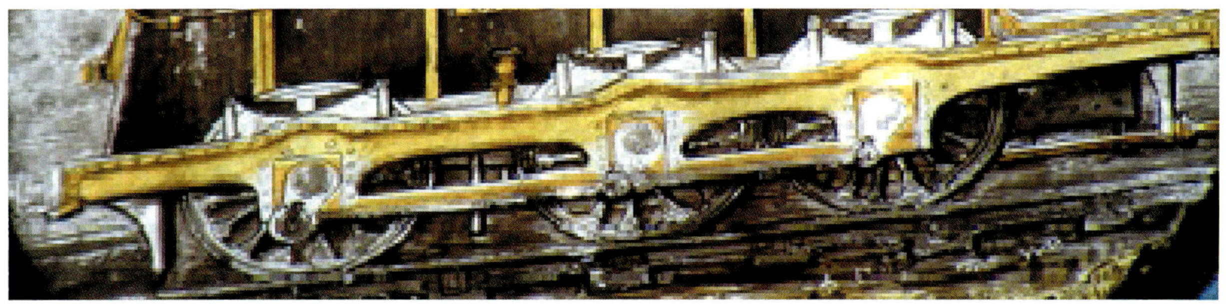

Watt's Steam Locomotive

Firstly, the wheels appear to be fixed with no piston rods attached to drive them. Maybe the point being made is that Watt may have refined and produced an engine but not a locomotive.

Secondly, the horizontal exposures of the crank handles appear on closest inspection to be 'eyes'.

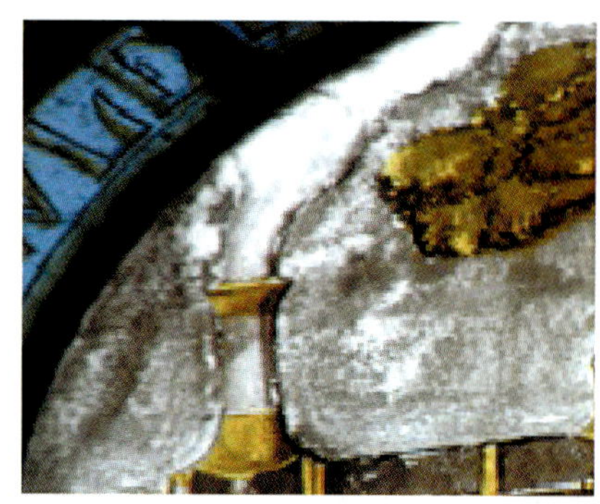

Thirdly, the steam coming from the funnel is clearly a face with its exaggerated nose poked down the funnel and eyes looking exclamatory.

Fourthly, there seem to be trees growing from the rear of the 'loco'!

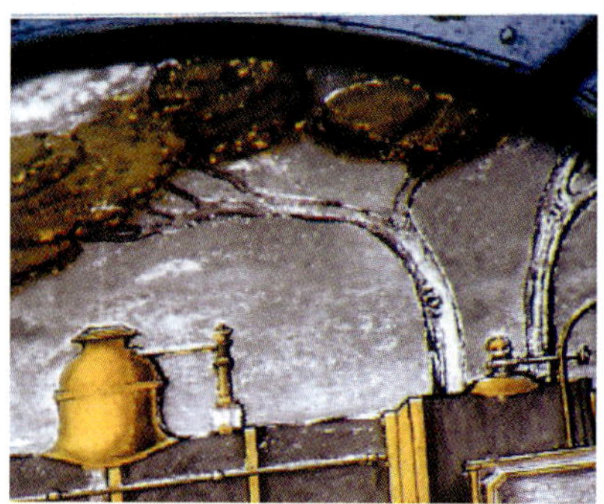

The legend chosen to accompany this 'header' is, so I am told spelled out in a Freemasons font. It is the choice of legend that is most thought provoking. The earliest record of its usage is attributed to Adam Smith, author of The Wealth of Nations but Francis Bacon used it in its Latin aphorism *Scientia Potentia est* in his *Meditationes Sacrae* in 1597.

Notably, Bacon was writing of God and the phrase is accurately translated as *'Knowledge is His Power'*. Former President of the USA, Thomas Jefferson used the phrase on two occasions most eloquently in a communication to a fellow politician that, [fellows should] *'possess information enough to perceive the important truths that knowledge is power, knowledge is safety, and that knowledge is happiness.*

More recently Kofi Annan was quoted as saying:

> *Knowledge is power, Information is liberating, Education is the premise of progress, in every society, in every family.*

Profound words were as important to Abraham Laverton as the bricks and mortar that built his institute.

d)   The Great Seal of Westbury (Header Panel Number 4)

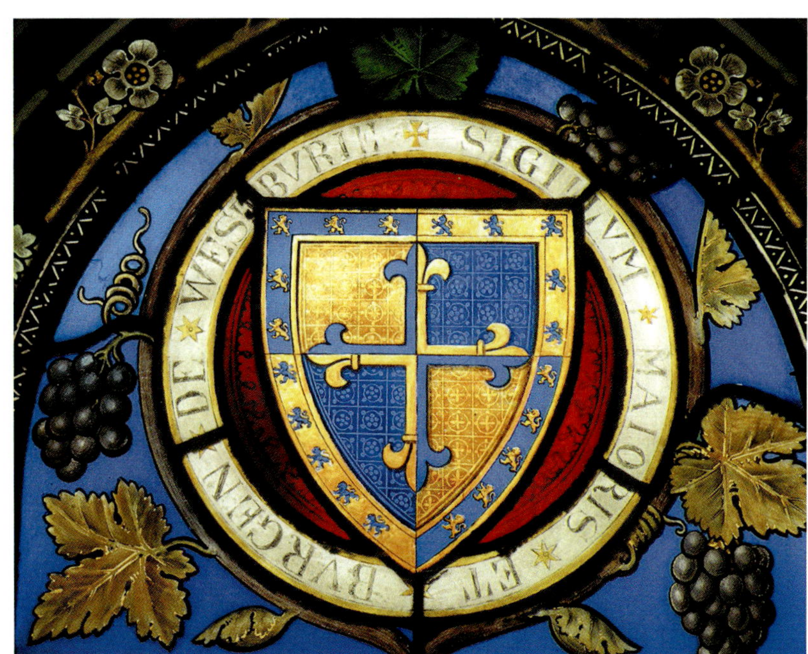

In this header the crest dates from the 19th century and has the Town's legend/motto for the time encircling its shield that is itself in the Town's colours.

Around the shield runs the lettering of the motto that in Latin says:

'*SIGILLUM MAIORIS ET BARGEN DE WESTBURIE*'

(that is slightly poor Latin, 'bargen' should read as 'burgensium')

It then translates as:

'The greater seal of the borough of Westbury'.

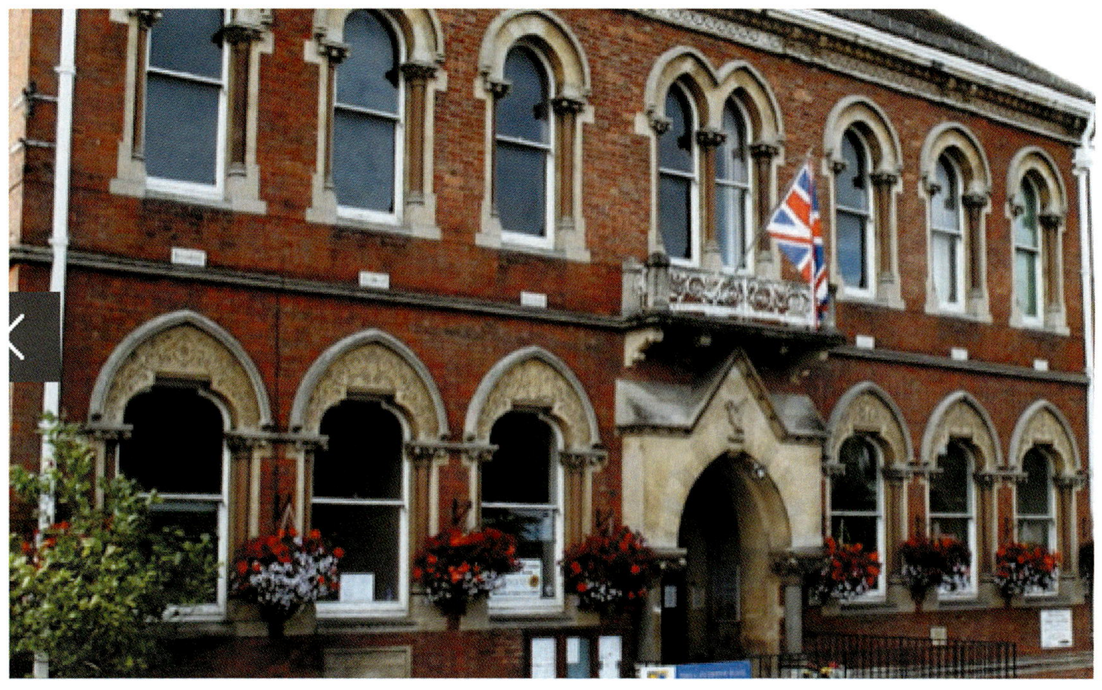

Outside of The Laverton Building today

The significance of this legend (not motto) is that it in fact dates back to the early Middle Ages. In its celebration of the 500th anniversary of the accession of Henry VIII to the Throne of England the National Archives describe the importance of seals as follows:

Seals were used to authenticate or validate documents, sometimes in place of a signature. They were also used to physically seal items of importance.

The term 'Great Seal' is given to seals used by monarchs, which were held in the custody of the Chancellor. A new Great Seal was made for each reign, with old seals ceremonially broken up once the reign had ended.

From the British Museum source relating to their former exhibition in January 2007 entitled

'Good impressions: image and authority in medieval seals'

Further explanation reads:

'the medieval period saw an unprecedented use of seals to validate legal documents and to protect personal correspondence . . . . royal, episcopal, ecclesiastic and aristocratic seals alongside those of towns and tradesmen [showed] how medieval people saw themselves.

In the Catalogue of Seals in the Department of Manuscripts at the British Museum, the work of Mr. Walter de Gray Birch, that for Westbury is as follows:

```
WESTBURY, CO. Wilts.

5485. [i6th cent] Sulph. cast from the matri.x. if x i|
in. [Ixxiii. 87.]

Oval : a shield of arms : quarterly, a cross, alternately
fleury and patonce, within a bordure charged with twenty
lioncels rampant, all counterchanged. Town OF Westbury.
Background coarsely hatched.

^ SIGILLVM Si MAIORIS » ET » BVRGEN » DE Ss WESTBVRIE.

Carved border, with four flowers in cross.

S. Lewis, Topogr. Did., vol. iv., p. 428.
```

There are many West Country places that carry the same provenance including the Castle of King Arthur at Tintagel where the legend was hung between the twin towers.

Chapter 9
Astronomy and the Window (The Four Asterisms)

Like many sixty-somethings I think I have a general knowledge of the night sky. Certainly, over the last ten years living on the edge of Salisbury Plain with a clear view to the Mendip Hills lying to the south-west and a slightly hazier, light-interrupted panorama of the Cotswolds to the west and north I have had plenty of opportunity to become familiar with the same ceiling of stars that Abraham Laverton would have sky-watched.

This was an important factor in my first recognising the layout of Ursa Major very easily in the third column of the Window even though that asterism was masked as a distribution of white flowers. Orion's belt gave that asterism away in the first column whilst the Pleiades resembling a cluster of diamond-like quality were unlikely to be ignored in any amateur astronomer's stained glass scrapbook of favourites. The Pleiades are in the fourth column. (Note, an asterism is a cluster of stars: Greek for star is *aster)*.

Of everything in the Window that caused a headache the main distribution of acorns and leaves in the twelve panes of the second column was the most painful. Both acorns and oak leaves are ancient symbols in this country of loyalty and nationalistic fervour and that had led me up various garden paths searching for patterns and reasoning. At the end of the day it came down to common sense.

Abraham Laverton had been familiar with the same constellations as any present-day citizens of the town, the best viewing for any amateur astronomer night on night being Ursa Major, Orion and the Pleiades as spectacles in the night sky. After these have been accounted for there are several other possibilities for the asterism in the remaining column. There is one particular candidate for consideration (given the local geography, light pollution and clarity of elevation) that is outstanding: Andromeda.

Lo and behold, when the distribution of the richest fruit of triple acorns are plotted the star Almach sits out like a beacon on its own above Newton's head whilst the stars Mirach and Alpheratz are markers below it. The inclusion of 'stars' by the Window's designer is selective and topographical but the pattern is there.

Whether Abraham Laverton discriminated between his astronomical, astrological and other interests in the night sky is unknown. Later consideration of solar and lunar eclipses are obviously discretely astronomical but they also get hijacked by less conventional parties of thought. Nevertheless, the four asterisms in the window tell us a good deal about the man.

An overview of the constellations of the night sky in the northern hemisphere is to be found on a following page and the asterisms we have interest in may be located. The non-astronomer must remember that the night sky is a dynamic sky that changes by the moment. An object may move a great distance in the night sky over a few hours and even disappear below the horizon. Every movement of a star or planet is relative to every other one and since Abraham Laverton's day some constellations have changed their configuration. The example of Orion's belt referred to following is such a case although that was over several thousands of years.

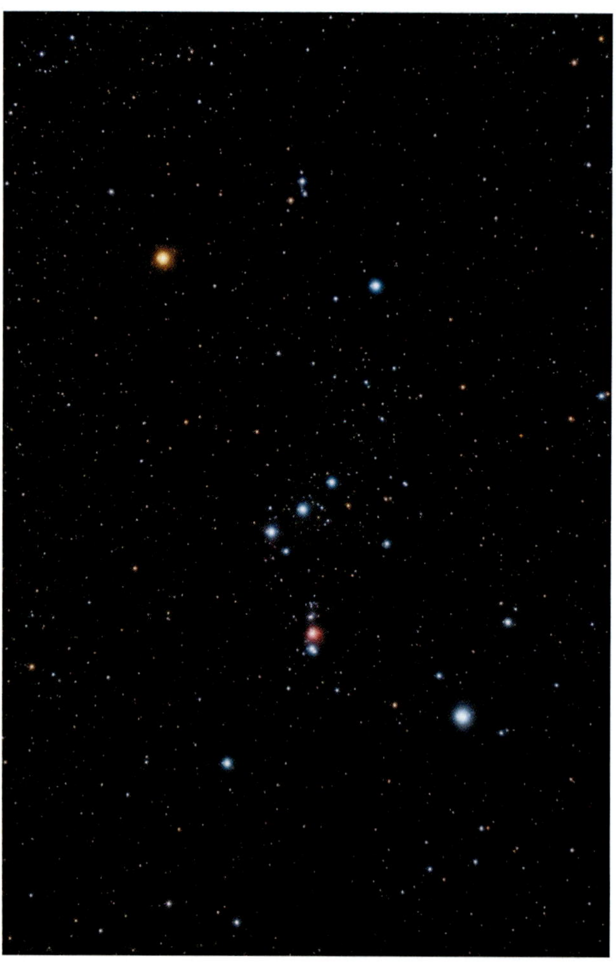

The Constellation of Orion featuring M42 & M43

The constellation of Orion is one of the most distinct star formations in the night sky. If a constellation can be described as popular this most romantic of star groups is just that and has at its centre the highly recognisable asterism of Orion's Belt.

The belt presently appears as a line of three stars but that was not always the case, a fact that has some bearing on the interpretation of what this window holds. The ancient Egyptians called it Sahu meaning the soul of Osiris.

In the winter months when it is visible in the northern hemisphere above the celestial equator even a modest telescope reveals that it contains a number of nebulae including M42, an 'object' that lies 1,500 light years away but may be seen from Earth with the naked eye.

Every major feature of this constellation has legends and mythology embracing it and the Hubble telescope showed what stunning features there are, such as the horsehead nebula.

In the Shakespeare column of the Window's panes stars from Orion are strung out from top to bottom but the belt is the giveaway.

The casual observer may also note that in the panes in which the belt occurs there is a dog-leg in the design. The three stars in question are not straight in line. This tells us that the source used in the design of the Window was not contemporary with that of its construction in the early 1870s It dates back in time to approximately 1,320 years BC when those stars were to be seen in that kind of alignment. For all that this may seem unlikely it in fact makes a good deal of sense if Abraham Laverton was a member of one of the brotherhoods written about earlier, the Rosicrucians or the Freemasons.

Both of these groups were sourced for many of their practices by ancient civilisations including those of Egypt, Sumeria, Chaldea, Amalekites and Assyria. All kinds of materials were passed down through lines of communication now long gone. If the Holy Grail can be traced to West Wales in the 20th Century then the only constraint on the impossible being possible here is the imagination.

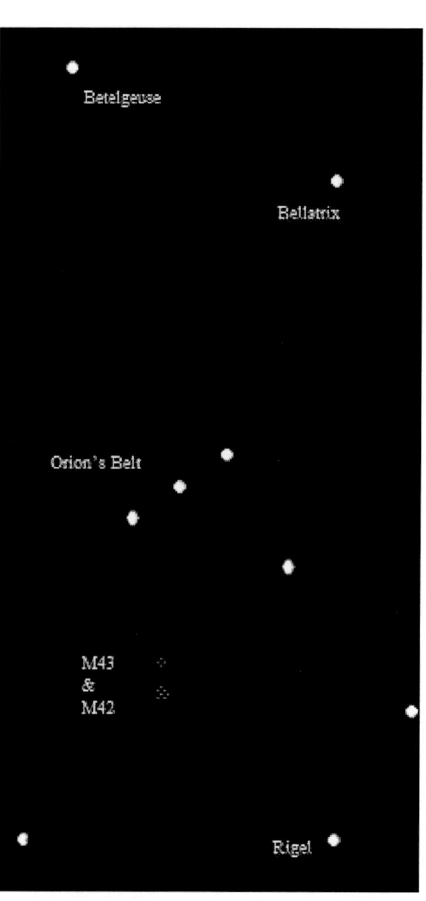

Photograph taken from Westbury.

It certainly takes imagination to try and see how some of the images used fit into the endless stories told. Mythmakers of ancient Greece and Rome as well as astrologers fit a young Hunter to this star formation. In truth any investigation could give any name to any celestial body and indifference and apathy would shine through upon them.

As mentioned earlier only four of the known constellations occur by name in the Bible and that was a sure influence for Laverton including them in the Window. On the other hand they have no particular attributes warranting their inclusion except for the Pleiades that is an asterism like no other. It is in the Book of Job where the words are found:

'Canst thou bind the sweet influence of the Pleiades or loose the bands of Orion?'

It is impossible to know what Abraham Laverton was thinking when he created such elaborate backdrops to the four columns of the Westbury Window. Why did he create such starry designs when constellations lend themselves so poorly to the task? Why did he choose such obvious asterisms without any notable moral or lesson to be taught or learned from them? Why try and disguise them if the point was to moralise anyhow?

Contradictions abound and all answers to these kind of questions are speculative. Given that the constellations are dressed as vegetation of one kind or another, do any of those plants have pertinent characteristics? It was mentioned earlier what the traditional meaning of the acorn was, so could there be any other significant symbolism?

The first thing I recognised when I viewed the Window in the Function Room of the Laverton Building in Westbury was the familiar pattern of the asterism of Ursa Major, also known as the Plough or Big Dipper, masked in the form of a distribution of white flowers in the third column from the left in the Window.

The second and third things were the belt of Orion in the first column and Pleiades in the fourth column. I thought the eclipse data was pretty obvious and the placements of each of the heads of the personages as the moons in each of the eclipses equally so.

As representations of celestial distributions in the night sky these asterisms were not configured with total accuracy. The designerclearly plotted some key reference points and shapes to be easily recognisable even though topologically misshapen. It does not mean that any of those distributions is much like what may be observed in the night sky but like most everything else in the Window is symbolic. The adaptation of 3D data to 2D paper or electronic multimedia means there will be some unavoidable inaccuracy, omission or compromise in presentation.

In this case as in the Shakespeare and Watt panes of the Window in order to present the data at all both shape and scale have been distorted. It is the third image of the constellation that retains its integrity the best and like Abraham Laverton it is that I most relate to. It is closest to being what I see in the Night Sky over Westbury more than five quarter centuries since he died.

The story of Andromeda in Greek Mythology is that of Cassiopeia, her father, boasting how much more beautiful she was than the daughters of the Sea God Poseidon. Poseidon was a sensitive soul so kidnapped Andromeda, chained her to a rock (the way you do) and waited for the sea monster Cerus to turn up for lunch.

The cunning plan was spoiled when our hero Perseus on a flying horse called Pegasus beamed into town, snatched Andromeda back and took her off to get married. They lived happily ever and Cerus had his take-away taken away.

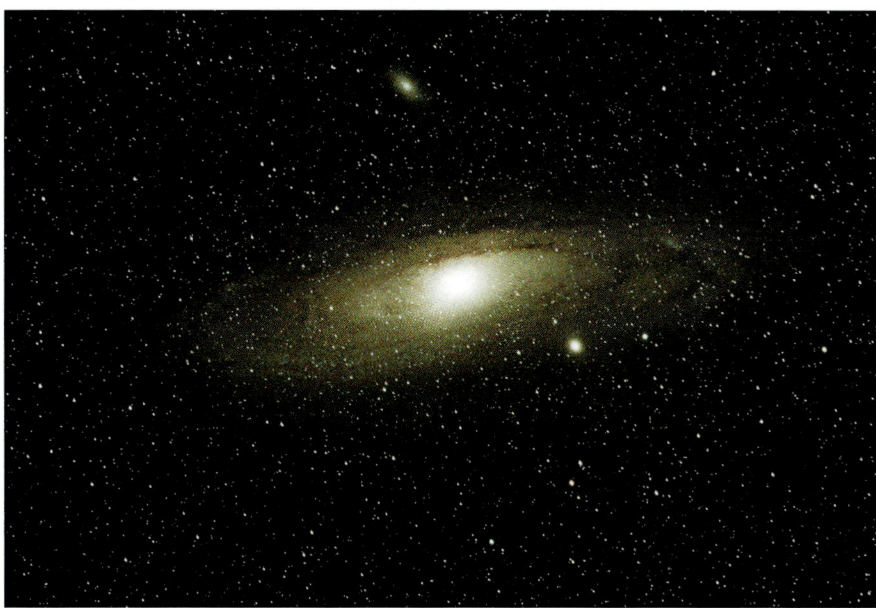

The Andromeda spiral

Within the Westbury Window it seems that the brighteer objects (as in Andromeda) occur where the richest fruit occurs such as triple acorns.

This matches up pretty well a quadrilateral of stars that includes Almaak and Mirach and leaves a fitting tail extending to Alpheratz and beyond.

It is noted that in the diagrams here the stars held to be in Andromeda actually overlap adjacent asterisms and do not necessarily fall neatly or conveniently onto a sheet of paper.

It is not recorded whether Abraham Laverton owned a telescope but with his wealth, his interests and his history he surely would have done. His last home at Farleigh Castle near Bath would have been an ideal place to pursue this interest with little atmospheric or light pollution. The night sky today is little dfferent to what Laverton would have observed over Westbury.

Ursa Major is the third largest constellation in the night sky and has for curious reasons been seen by many civilisations as resembling a bear. Others have seen it as a wagon, a big dipper, a plough or a sheep fold. As constellations go it is relatively close to our solar system and is classified as a cluster. Because it is close it appears scattered over a relatively large area of the night sky.

In the same field of vision that the sky watcher views Ursa Major there is also an extensive field of galaxies that makes it an interesting place to study. Ursa Major is a very useful directional finder with the two stars in the plough's bowl furthest from its handle pointing towards the North Pole Star whilst the curved handle itself points towards the bright star Arcturus.

Spiral galaxies, pin-wheel galaxies and cigar galaxies are to be found in Ursa Major. Myths and stories about the Great Bear abound and it has been important in Greek, Roman and Chinese mythologies.

The constellation of Ursa Major viewed from Westbury

If there is a lesson to be learned from the consideration of these star groups it is that the interpretation of what they represent is cultural and conditioned by societal values. For example, one asterism within this constellation is known in cultures of Arabic descent as 'Three Leaps of Gazelle', not something that easily comes to mind if viewing this particular constellation from a Scottish croft let alone rural Wiltshire.

Theosophical beliefs in north-west Europe relate the Seven Sisters of the Pleiades and their spiritual energy being transfered in the most unsubstantiated way to find their place in all mankind through the Masters of the Seven Rays. Growing up in the valleys of South Wales this appears to be something I missed out on but Abraham Laverton had a realisation of some relevance here.

The word bear is also a euphemism for totally different things away from a large mammal or a series of stars. The term 'bear market' has a meaning on the world's financial markets quite alien from the two aforementioned meanings. As an investor in the country's industries, particularly the railways, Abraham Laverton would have been very interested in any bear of good fortune.

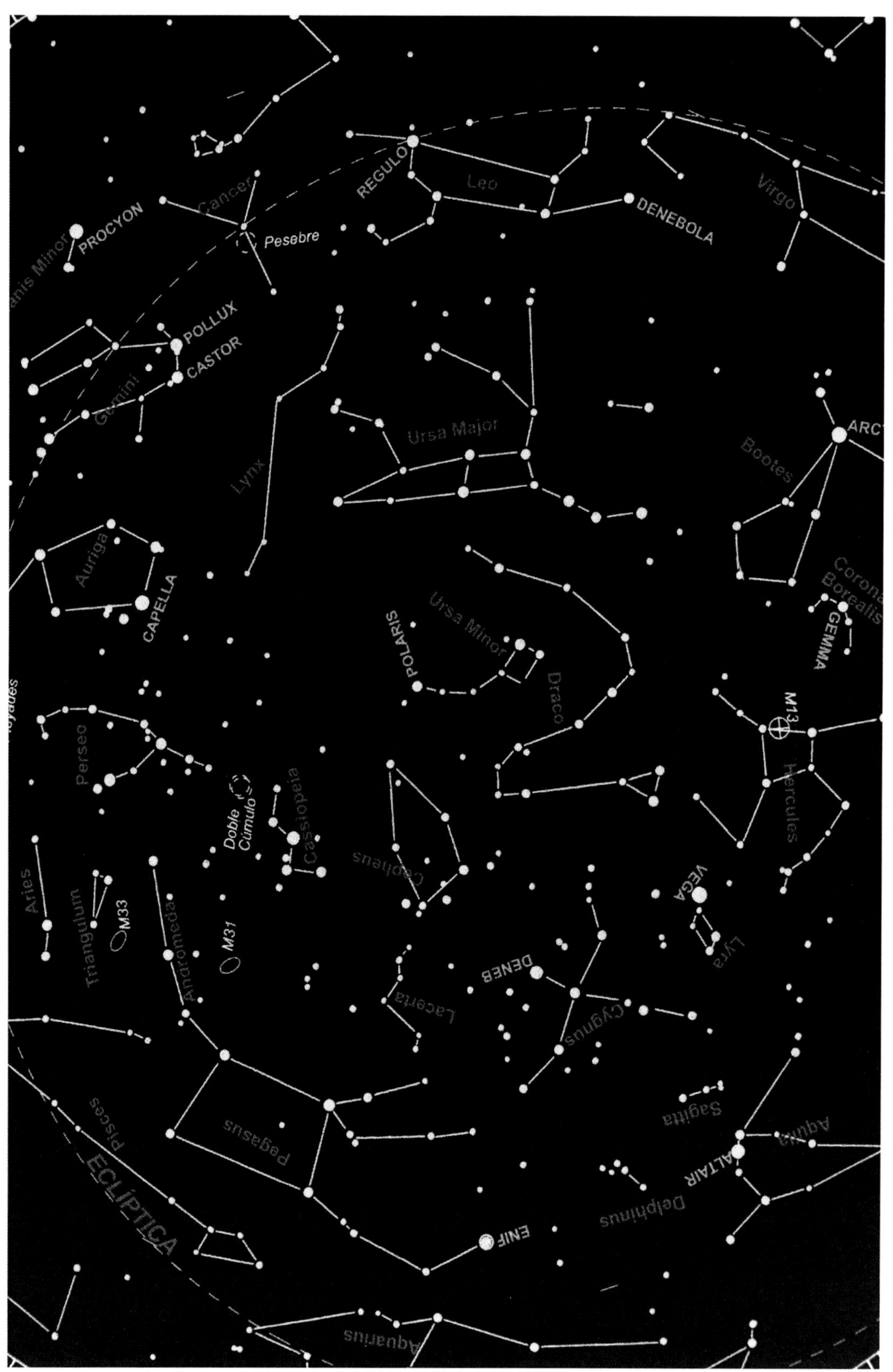

Constellations of the Night Sky in the Northern Hemisphere

The Pleiades is one of the smallest constellations in the night sky. The column of glass panes in the fourth section of the window are occupied by imagery associated with this asterism. The Pleiades, also known as the Seven Sisters, lies in the constellation of Taurus.

The stars of The Pleiades are surrounded by dust like matter that reflects the blue light of the stars. This is difficult to see below but in the inset adjacent to the inverted colour image of the asterism there is at least one star demonstrating this. Alcyone is a Blue White giant lying 378 light years away.

Whatever the Pleiades were seen as by Abraham Laverton there is an ugly side to the imagery he sanctioned. Edwin Landseer was not a well man and some might argue that he was not a nice man either. It is well documented that he had problems with alcohol, drugs and depression and died the year the Laverton Institute opened in 1873.

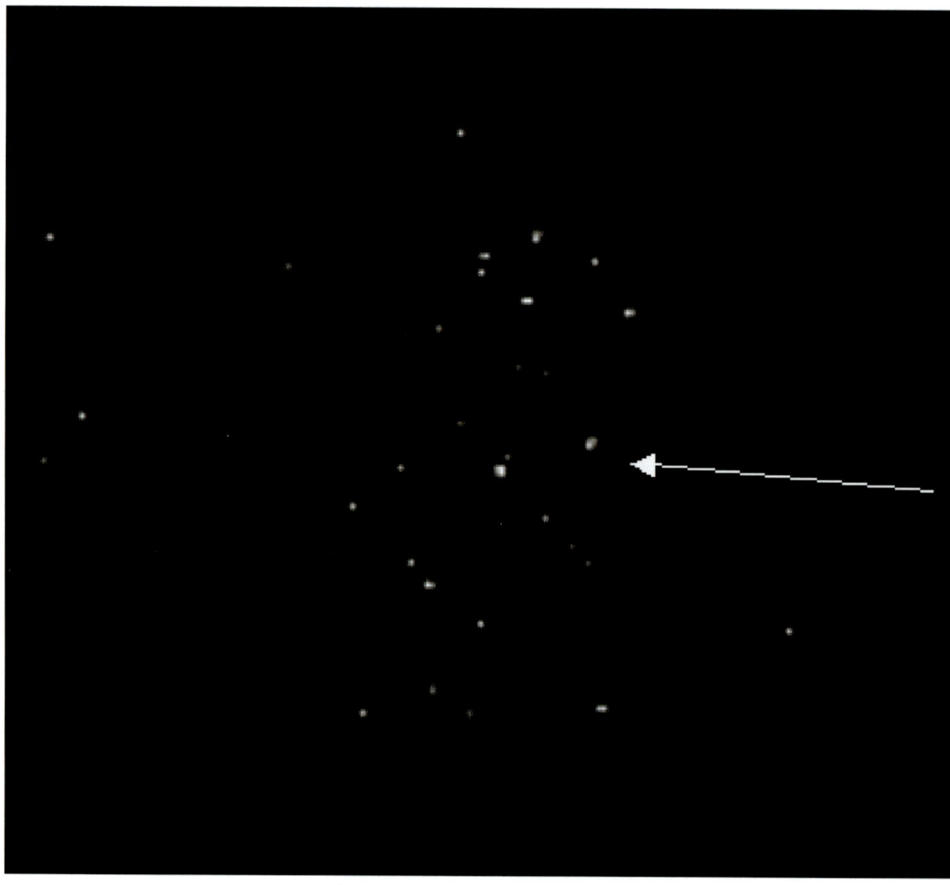

The Pleiades from Westbury, photograph taken with a point and shoot hand held camera.

Pointed at by an arrow is the star Alcyone that shines 1400 times brighter than our sun.

The number and distribution of the stars in the Pleiades is a matter of conjecture and determined by the quality of the observer's telescope. There is a great deal of mysticism associated with this asterism. Many early societies have been enchanted, bemused or admiring of it from the Chinese to the Australian aboriginals, from the Maya, to the Sioux, from the Japanese to the Aztecs. Mentioned in both Homer's Iliad and Odyssey, the Pleiades are noted in the Bible, revered in Hindu mythology and are so much part of Japanese culture too.

Chapter 10
Total Solar and Lunar Eclipses

Interviewing people in Westbury about the Window and asking them whether they knew about it, and what they knew about it, showed up some interesting degrees of accuracy of perception. Some recounted totally inaccurate information, some related intimate experiences (usually a wedding reception), some recalled a memorable meeting but rarely did anyone recount a fact, or a revelation or an anecdote.

Everyone seems to know the Window exists and a surprisingly high frequency of brides remembered the colourful backdrop it provided on their big day whether five or fifty years ago. In the past I have mentioned that I believed that more men would be cognizant of it than women. It seems more the case that men are less inhibited about voicing complete nonsense where women are more reluctant to risk embarrassment should they mislead me. They prefer to carefully drip-feed information before freely revealing their hand-me-down histories.

For more than fifteen minutes I listened to one man talk about his substantial knowledge of the Window before being liberated from his company. I knew he knew a lot about the Window because he introduced himself with the words *'I know a lot about this window'*, before impressing myself and the attendant company with his appraisal of the four celebrated representatives of the Arts and Sciences in Britain, Wordsworth, Stephenson, Brunel and Turner. I have still to discover where that window is.

What the Window is all about does not sit easily with a few of those citizens who have lived long lives in the town. Whereas the thirty- and forty-somethings dismiss any ignorance with a joke and some self-deprecating humour other 'locals' have seemed to regard ignorance as weakness. This monument in their lives seems to have cast a shadow through which the only beams of light come from reciting the mantra about the four celebrated achievers and pointing out a couple of coats of arms.

This fact is important because there are doubtless many more life-long residents who do not have a clue about what the Window contains and when they cannot express any knowledge confidently about it then they do not talk about it. A vicious circle of suppressing information was set in motion 140 years ago by Abraham Laverton who created a tribute to his own brilliance along with that of William Jervis Stent that simply has been too difficult to crack for most of the townspeople most of the time. So, it has been ignored.

It happens. More than thirty years ago I attended a guided tour of a major northern city as part of a week of events to celebrate that city's architectural heritage. The leader of the tour, a much celebrated architect and national figure, began his walk and talk with the line:

> 'It amazes me that anyone has bothered to turn up this morning because your city is an architectural desert'.

By lunchtime he was talking to himself. He had alienated his audience from the time he first drew breath and likewise the Window does not have an audience of followers today because it has never had an audience of followers. Everything that Laverton placed in this masterpiece is lost because it is such a chore to decipher and decode.

There is probably not a Window, nor a wall, nor a façade, nor anything quite like it in the country or maybe the world. It is remarkable and deserves an interested and educated audience. That does not mean that one needs to have passed examinations at school in order to appreciate what the Window is all about. A simple outline of information might be made available to younger children, increasing in quality and depth to a mature selection of information giving the main facts to interested adults.

For all that has been stated so far the foundation structure of the Window embraces astronomy as its fundamental reason for being. Astronomy is not taught in our schools in any meaningful way so if the Window is to be popularly understood then appreciation of it must come from it being promoted and publicised separately. Organisations such as the Town Council have a major part to play. I am modest fan of theirs and acknowledge their superb cooperation in enabling this book to be crafted and the Window to be explored.

The appropriate astronomical nous is not particularly about asterisms or constellations but begins with the phenomenon of the eclipse. The whole structure of the Window is based upon an understanding of an eclipse, total or partial, solar or lunar.

I repeat the point that each of the four heads of the personages 'celebrated' in the Window is positioned as would be the Earth's moon in the event of a total eclipse of the Sun. Behind their heads are the bulbous prominences of solar activity that may occur during such an event.

Bordering each of the prominences are eight sets of suns that almost seem to be decorative rather than anything else. At the corners of each main inset are four green spheres of what may be seen to be moon-like or earth-like proportions compared to the obscured suns. Their colouring varies around Shakespeare's head with one darker green and three lighter green, around Newton two are darker and two are lighter, around Watt three are darker and one is lighter, whilst around Landseer all four are darker green.

The obvious thinking here is that these green spheres represent the moon at different stages of its monthly cycle and that may be so. However when first considering this possibility something seemed curious about the numbers involved here. The number of suns in pairs of eight around each personage and lining the prominences is 64 whilst the number of suns around the whole of each personage's insert varies as (including filling in the blanks) 81, 81, 83 and 83.

These struck me as significant at a very terrestrial level because from the choir singing days of my youth I recall a music conductor who tutored some friends and myself in singing a cappella that there is a thing called 'just' or 'pure' intonation in music. He forever made the point that there is little difference between music and noise and that unless we maintained correct pitch and duration in expressing a note as expounded by Pythagorean tuning then we would be making noise and not music.

Pythagoras was a believer in and advocate of the healing properties of music and employed melodies against rage and anger as well as less abstract physical phenomena. His approach to this was based on the idea that the frequency intervals of sound are as aesthetically tuned as possible approximating a ratio of 3:2 and the most common criterion understood for that at the time was 81:64. This was called the Pythagorean major-third but its shortcoming was that it limited musicians from using triads and chords.

On a twelve tone scale using Pythagorean tuning the unstable interval ratio of 81 over 64 produces a 'C' (major) that is not the optimum pitch for some but suits singing A cappella or playing bagpipes, flute, violin or trombone. The obvious questions raised are 'was there a musical dimension to the design of the Window?' Further, are there harmonics functioning as background to the eclipse phenomenon?

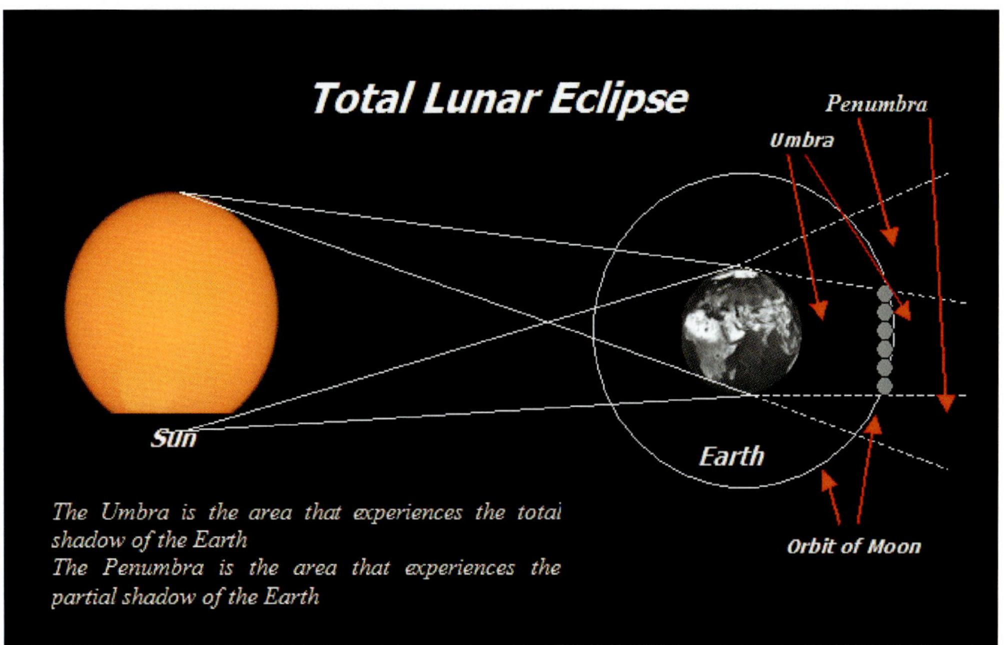

The diagram above shows the positions of the Sun, the Moon and the Earth in the event of a Total Lunar Eclipse

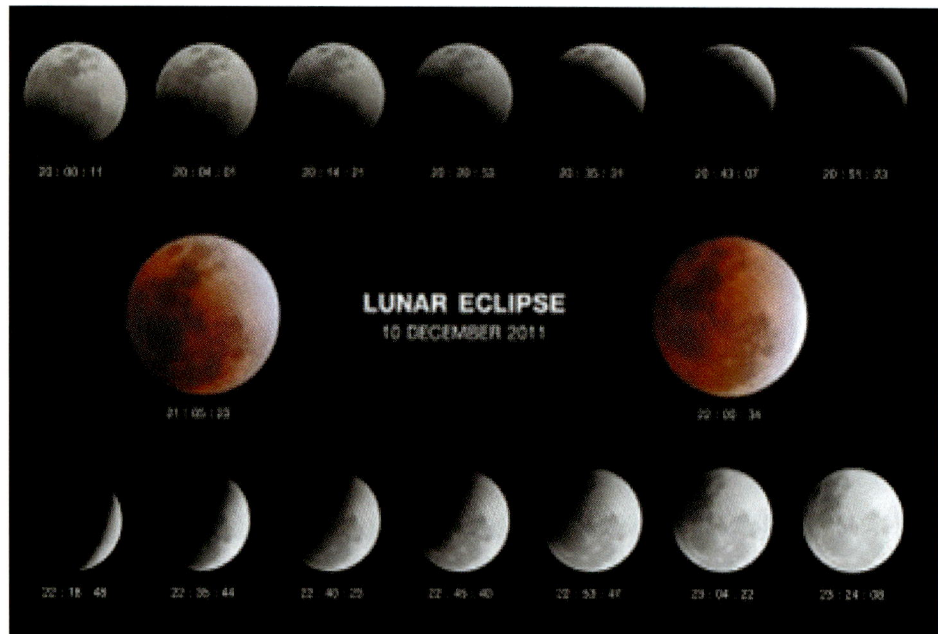

Photographs in series of a Lunar Eclipse

Without wishing to be distracted from the significance of the eclipse within the design of the Window there is more to be considered here. When considering what to include in these writings I initially thought I initially thought that there would be a watershed between what I can relate to when putting pen to paper and what I feel needs a disclaimer that will divorce myself from some of the bizarre things that people once believed. Esoteric, occult, cabbalistic, theosophic brotherhoods or not some of the content that follows I cannot in good faith give any credence to. In the context of the Window I will attempt to give them a respectable airing.

How Abraham Laverton saw the overlap between astronomy and astrology is one question that arises. The phenomena of solar and lunar eclipses are represented in the Window against a backdrop of beliefs that date back to Pythagoras and before. He related the existence of what he termed musical harmonies that resounded through the cosmos at frequencies based on laws of mathematics.

He was not alone in doing this. The Chinese, the Hindus, the Persians and the Egyptians had done the same or similar in relation to their ceremonials at which 'music' was played but not with the credibility of a mathematical foundation. What Pythagoras worked out was the existence of what he called the music of the spheres the superior of which he termed Limitless and Eternal Life, something that Abraham Laverton as an alchemist would have been deeply interested in.

The sun is the major player in all this and to the Sphere of Equality Pythagoras assigned a tone, harmonic interval, name, number, colour and form. He did this for all natural phenomena in the Universe such as planets, constellations and elements. For the relationships between each he established harmonic ratios that have become the basis of the science of modern music.

For the structure of these harmonic ratios Pythagoras hypothesised grades of energy and substance symbolised as pyramid structures that interacted with each other and music of the spheres according to a specific definition or plan that maintains the Universe. Integral to this is the concept of two further pyramids: one representing Fire and one representing Earth. Obeying the law of elemental harmony Fire and Earth do not enter each other's composition.

In the Westbury Window the astronomical phenomenon of the eclipse, the mathematical foundation of musical frequencies, the concept of harmonic ratios, an applied structure of elemental forces enhancing the spheres of equality all come together in a pot-pourri of pseudo-science. The structure of green moons or rosettes that either orbit or encircle each of the heads of the four personages demonstrates this.

Reflecting again on the Window the spheres (moons or rosettes) around Shakespeare's head represent Air, those around Newton and Watt respectively represent the Sphere of Equality and Fire whilst the head of Landseer is surrounded by the symbols for Earth. These were believed to be four of the five basic elements that made up the world.

It happens that the ratios between these elemental components make various harmonies that added up make a diapason harmony or octave. In the progression of harmonic ratios the octave is the interval between two musical notes one of which has twice the pitch of the other and lies eight notes away from it counting inclusively along the diatonic scale.

This was all as much philosophy as science to Pythagoras in his time. He was in pursuit of musical harmonies for the cure of ailments of the spirit and the body. Like many others at this time Laverton wanted everlasting life and whilst he knew that Pythagoras' 'science' was more musical medicine than it was mathematics these were times when astronomical reality and astrological superstition merged in a very fuzzy way.

What the Window presents to the viewer is an overlap of representations. Laverton uses the Pythagorean structure to present his perception of solar and lunar eclipses. He has bracketed in the Window its' circumferences of suns in groups of five, each of which totals 80 and with the suns behind each personage total, 81 and 81, giving the value to calculate the ratio for a major chord 'C'.

For Shakespeare and Landseer this harmonious state is not realised as sums add up to 83 and 83.

Taking this into account these data items get even fuzzier in their significances as the inharmonious nature of the ratios consequently generated produce discord. Was this the point that Laverton was trying to make candidly about the lives of Shakespeare and Landseer.

Given the intellectual turmoil in which Newton led his life it is difficult to credit any such selective criticism. For all his genius Newton spent his life in no state of equilibrium but by futile searches to find meaning in all sorts of weird, off the wall, occult practices. He tried to extract scientific information from the Bible, he was obsessed with extracting the sacred wisdom from the Temple of Solomon, he toyed with the sacred geometry of golden sections and cosmic spirals, he endlessly searched for dissertations on alchemy and became a great admirer of Joseph Mede a professed prophetic interpreter of the Bible. In short he wasted much of his time on mystic nonsense in a manner it is now easy to sneer at.

Abraham Laverton was also between two stools and his placing of the lunar eclipse as a classical event or a purely astronomical one appears to have been unresolved.

The solar eclipse is included in the Window's design more as a token gesture than a meaningful statement. In Victorian Britain there was a fascination about the idea of a total solar eclipse. From the year 1724 to 1925 there was no total eclipse over a populated or accessible land area of Britain. The last in 1724 had followed a north-west to south-east track from southern Wales and Devon to the south-east and Kent.

The next to occur was on 24th January 1925 over territorial waters north of the Hebrides. It reached no land. It was not until 29th June 1927 that 24 seconds of totality occurred across the south coast of England but that was spoiled by weather dominated by dense cloud and high winds.

On 30th June 1954 there was a total solar eclipse over Unst in the Shetlands and on 16th February 1961 a maximum eclipse was observed on the horizon in parts of the north of Scotland. The total solar eclipse over Cornwall and parts of south Devon on 11th August 1999 was much more than the event of a lifetime and for Abraham Laverton it would have been of massive significance.

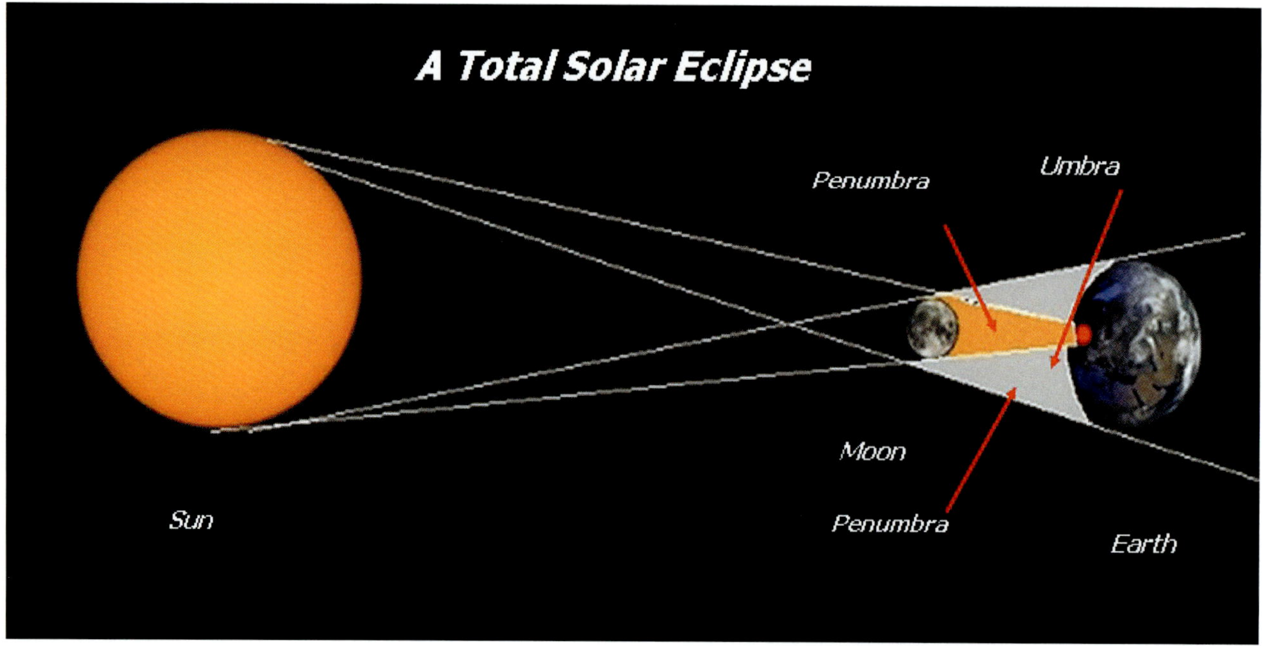

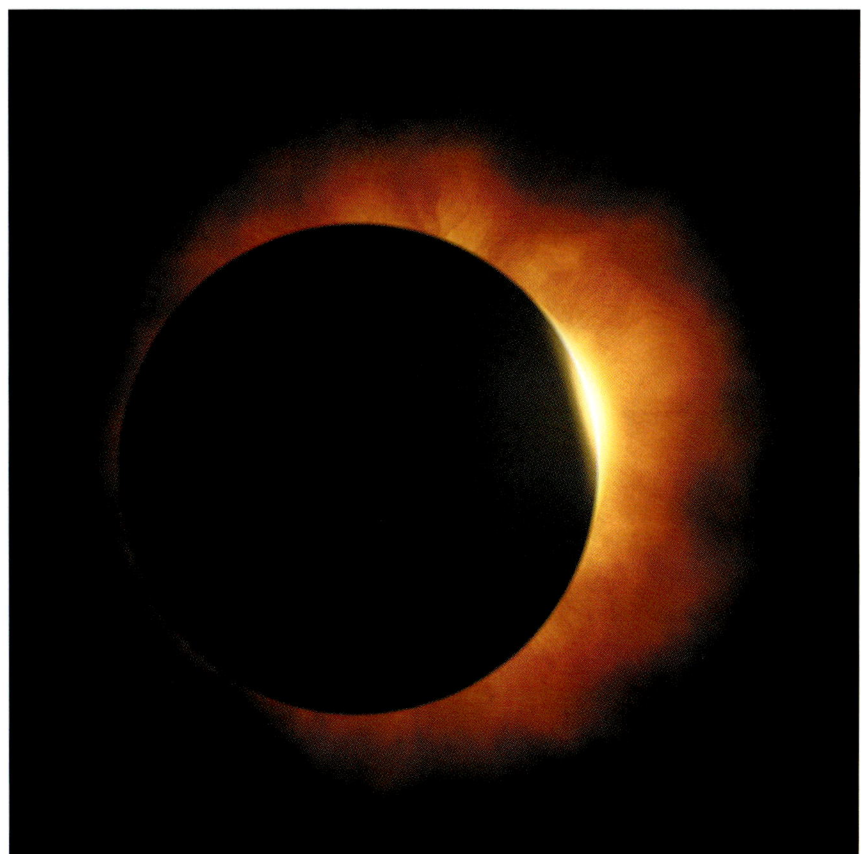

Photograph of a Total Solar Eclipse with 'diamond ring' effect

The occurrence of a total solar eclipse anywhere in the world of the Victorians was a significant or even an epoch-making event. Courtesy of the Chaldeans, a people from an ancient region of Babylonia, the times, dates and tracks of eclipses were known well and predicted with great accuracy and confidence. The Chaldeans called the system the Saros and it was structured on observations of recurrent cycles of eclipses every 6585.3 days or just over every 18 years. It applied to both lunar and solar eclipses

There were observed to be many more than one of these cycles and they varied (and still do) in their frequency according to the measurement of synodic, anomalistic or draconic data. These terms refer to respective periods from New Moon to New Moon, perigee to perigee and Draconic node to node. Most people lead their lives oblivious to this and never give a thought to these geometries. Abraham Laverton was not such a man and gave it considerable thought.

Just as the NASA space organisation still uses the Saros as its guide to when both solar and lunar eclipses will occur so clearly did Abraham Laverton understand the prerequisites for both solar and lunar events. For example it is apparent from the Window that he had the three objects lined up and a full moon passing close to the ecliptic plane (the vertical centre lines of each vertical set of twelve panes). Considering he was essentially producing a work of art this was a clever token gesture and equally as well considered as another piece of physics that he seems to make recognition of, namely Kepler's First Law of Motion.

Laverton knew that the perfectionists, astronomers, astrologists et al would be looking to be hypercritical about any howlers he made in the basic integrity of his design and one such obvious potential graphical faux pas was the fact that the circles of suns should not be perfect circles but ellipses whether they represent Moons, Earths or Suns. He again doubled up his artistic symbolism here by adding in for the circles around the heads of Shakespeare and Landseer two more suns than he has for the other two personages.

As three dimensional objects orbiting in four perceptible dimensions if their centres of gravity and their radii remain the same for two parts of an orbit but their radii vary greater or smaller for the other two parts then the shape of the orbit must be elliptical - with all the implications that has for varying velocity at perihelion, aphelion and the equinoxes. This makes for an imperfect circle and imparts an imperfect mathematical condition upon the already noted inharmonious classical ratios.

Typically Laverton was killing at least two birds with one stone, or planet. Considering that he was being sympathetic to the inclusion of data that was inclusive of Kepler's First Law of Motion I thought that he may well do so elsewhere in the Window as there are so many overlaps of data and multiple inclusions.

What were readily apparent were the vine patterns on the Window sections of Newton and particularly Watt that have loops and circles in abundance. They appear a little bit naïve in diagrammatic terms but comparing the bottom two panes of the Watt section with a typical textbook illustration of the time (though a little bit later) the representation of the Earth's orbit around the Sun with the Moon orbiting the Earth in the 'Project Gutenberg' eBook 'Aether and Gravitation' by William George Hooper published in 1903 there is a clear example of the ellipse paths as set out in the Window.

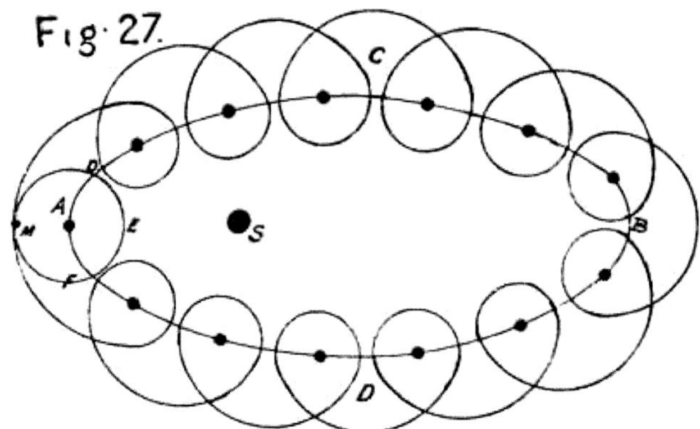

Above, Figure 27 from the Hooper book.
Orbits of Earth and the Moon around the Sun
And below similar patterns on the cover page of the Hooper book

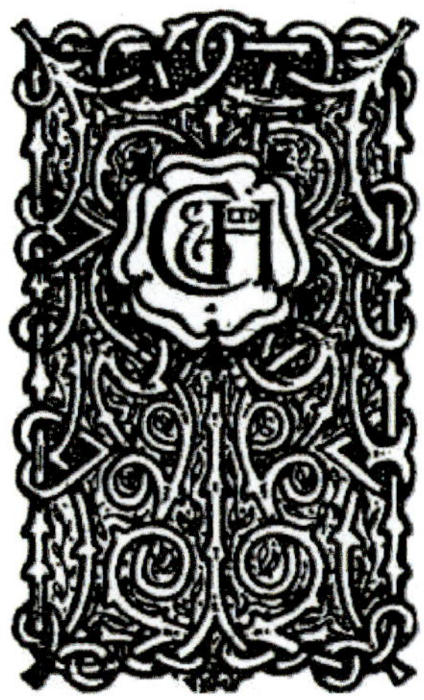

What is more, the graphic on the title page of that book has many of the same patterns and paths too.

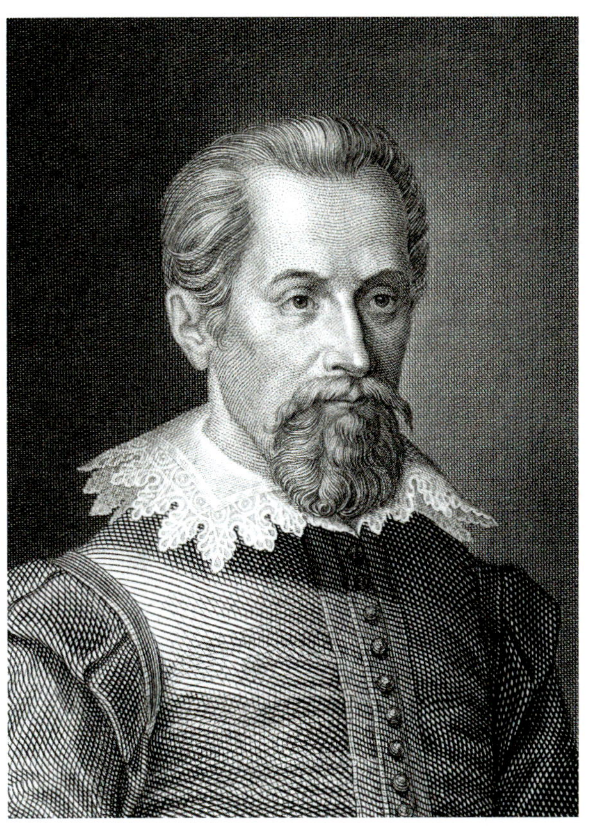

To the left is an image of Johannes Kepler. His laws of motion are fundamental to understanding the movements of the planets around the Sun and the Moon around the Earth.

These movements are shown throughout the Window as vine patterns as shown below.

Note Laverton has even plotted the twin focii about which an elliptical orbit takes place.

The diagram below illustrates some of the problems encountered when seeking an accurate representation of a planetary object. It is an excerpt taken from the Watt column in the Window and bares extraordinary similarity to the "Figure 27" from the Hooper book regarding, the shape and form of the vines.

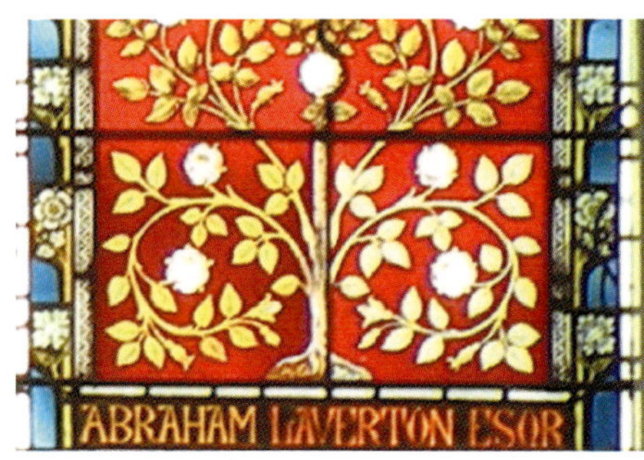

It is quite clear that Abraham Laverton was incorporating the basic principle of Kepler's First Law of Motion into his Stained Glass Window. He may not have been tagging it as that but in each of the loops of vine in the bottom two panes the two lower white flowers represent the reflected Sun as one of the two focal points that characterise any elliptical orbit.

Within the solar system the ellipse of any object orbiting the Sun has two focal points and the Sun is always one of them.

Kepler's ongoing work in the last decade of the sixteenth century largely focussed upon astronomical problems but he also considered their astrological consequences, the implication for weather systems on the planet and how they in turn influenced the harmonies between music and mathematics. Unfortunately much of his work was dogged by poor data and his reputation suffered accordingly though evidently not in the mind of Abraham Laverton nearly 300 years later.

Another obvious question that arises relates to whether or not Laverton managed to replicate accurately in the Window and to any scale the eccentricity of either the Moon's orbit around the Earth or that of the Earth around the Sun. The mathematics is a little intimidating but, like Kepler, anyone choosing to resolve the equation needs to be confident in the accuracy of their raw data components.

For the orbit of the Moon around the Earth where –

$$E = \sqrt{1 + \frac{2EL}{m_{red} \, \alpha^2}}$$

E=   Total Orbital Energy
L=   Angular Momentum
Mred= Reduce Mass

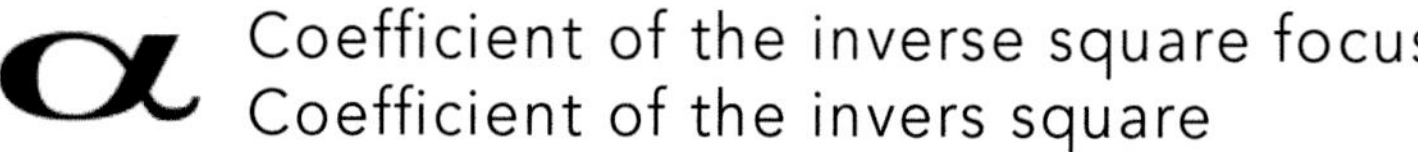

α Coefficient of the inverse square focus
Coefficient of the invers square

-focus, with example of central force being gravity.

The figure that emerges is deviant from the one set out as the real world eccentricity of orbit but in a work of art that is of no surprise. Fitting an accurate scaled model into a stone sculpted window is a little too much. Eccentricity of the Moon's orbit has a mean index of 0.0549; i.e it is very elliptical or non-circular.

Chapter 11

Rosicrucians, Freemasons and The Knights Templar

As reading and research for this book advanced so did the question as to whether or not Abraham Laverton was a Rosecrucian, Freemason or Knight Templar. It became more compelling with each revelation to try and determine what the motivation was for one man to spend so much time, money and intellectual endeavour to achieve the goal of installing the Window that he must have realised people may never see or understand.

From early on it seemed a possibility he was a member of the Rosicrucians, then a definite maybe, then an absolutely not, followed by he must have been and then despair at the mixed messages that the Window yielded. It was elsewhere that the answer was found in a much smaller and more modest piece of stained glass craftsmanship in the north wall of the parish church of All Saints, Westbury.

Finding out anything about the followers of the Rosy Cross is like trying to catch a leaf falling from a tree on a windy day. The Rosicrucians are so secretive the average person does not know they exist. The Freemasons aspire to the same anonymity but it was a tradition during the years of Abraham Laverton's 'watch' over the clandestine brotherhoods of Westbury that so long as he lived then the Rosicrucians would hold the alpha male status over their rivals.

What the Rosicrucians lay claim to, are the 'esoteric truths' that give insight into the physical universe and the spiritual realm according to the doctrine as set out by Christian Rosenkreuz during the first quarter of the seventeenth century. At least, that is the theory.

There is a strong body of opinion that contends that the Rosy Cross is no more than a fantasy with a school of pseudo-religious pretenders inventing their own Christian Mystics and attendant objects of devotion.

The icon that symbolises this 'most laudable order' is the Rosy Cross. This is a colourful almost childish-looking cross that bears no similarity to the Christian Cross and its whole ambience it at odds with the drab colourlessness of Lutheranism with which it has become most closely associated in the Protestant fold.

Its doctrinal teaching is most certainly at odds with Catholicism and is even more estranged from Islam. It shares common ground with Freemasonry and AMORC (Ancient Mystical Order of Rosae Crucis as it likes to be known) further contends it carries no religious baggage as it predates Christianity. Its iconic cross represents:

the unfolding consciousness of the individual in a challenging life well lived.

The followers of the Rosy Cross claim to adhere to a movement with its roots anchored in ancient Egypt. Some regard them as opportunists bound to a belief system that originates in the mystery schools of the Pharaoh Thutmose III (1500 BC - 1470 BC). They practise their art today presenting their history through mystical allegories passed down the centuries by word of mouth.

The first esoteric school of initiates was set up during the time of Thutmose III and was continued by Pharaoh Amenhotep IV whose legacy was passed down to the likes of Pythagoras in Greece and Plotinus in Rome though without the name by which it is now recognised.

Mystical knowledge and mystical teachings were attractions and given what is written so far in this chapter the phrase selected by Abraham Laverton for the header panel above James Watt, *"Knowledge is Power"*, takes on a far greater significance. In accordance with the spiritual realm of the physical universe (he would have believed in this if a Rosicrucian) then his philanthropy and benevolence towards his 'employees' were extensions of his intuitive theosophy. He did not employ workers, he employed people.

With this in mind the Rosy Cross is seen as a unifying 'power' in the organisation of the Great White Brotherhood that included the Templars and the Militia Crucifera Evangelica. Laverton would have been privy to extraordinary revelations and knowledge and Knowledge is . . . .

I reiterate my disclaimer to having any personal interest in this weird Victorian world and am only trying to put the content of the Window in context. Also if the reader has reached thus far in this book without first taking at least an hour out with something like Al Seckel's *'Incredible Visual Illusions'* then you are unlikely to appreciate where Abraham Laverton was coming from.

In a world where most people had not the ability to understand the written word visual imaging was a major means of communication and there were endless means of trickery employed to confuse or trick the less able. The Rosicrucians were intense users of visual imaging for clandestine propaganda and in the north wall stained glass window of the All Saints parish church dedicated to Laverton is to be seen a host of concealed letters spelling out coded messages in Freemason's *script (Examples are shown below).*

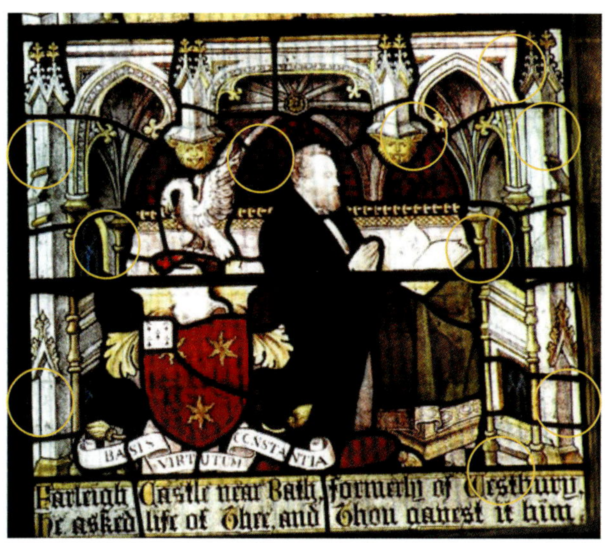

Identifiable Freemasons symbols or letters include those circled below. Translated they include *y, s, s ,y, u, t, t,* and the means to do this is on a score of Internet sites.

As a follower of the Rosy Cross Abraham Laverton had access to the mystical early teachings of the Brotherhood before it was reinvented around the fifteenth century. He was able to draw on its earliest texts or oral tradition dating back to the Second Millennia BC in Egypt. A graphic produced in 1492 illustrates Pythagoras experimenting with weights to produce music (reprinted on page 31 of the Rosicrucian Digest Number 1 in the year 2009). This refers to events that occurred in the fifth century BC but is accompanied by a signature cartouche from a thousand years later that is the mark of one Tutankhamun, ruler in Egypt during the 18th dynasty. (see below)

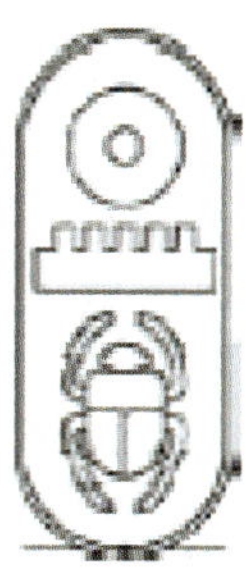

Pythagoras' experiments were noted earlier but in it's margin another graphic may be seen that is unmistakeably similar to that following here –

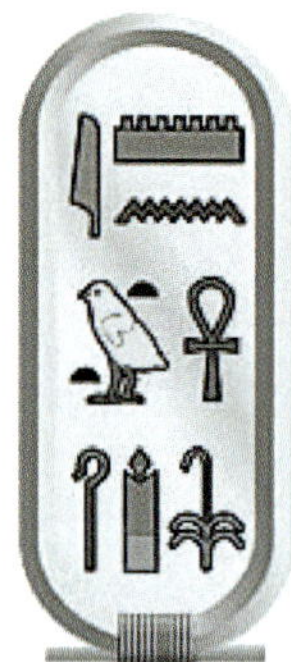

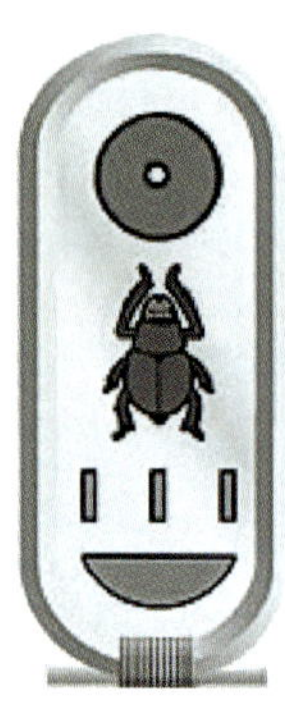

The name Tutankhamun was the first title of the Boy King and meant *'Living Image of Amun'*, his divine name.

It is this second cartouche that identifies the scarab beetle below the sun. In association with the universal Sky God below it was the royal acknowledgement of King Tutankhamun .

It is this identity that is also found eluded to in the margin of the 15th century graphic of Pythagoras, an identity that if one visits Egypt today one will find everywhere as the mark of the celebrated Boy King.

Can the Rosicrucians have had 'knowledge' dating so far back that there is/was association with Tutankhamun regarding the origin of mystical writings and teachings? Abraham Laverton may have believed that to be so and sensed substantial power from being so privileged.

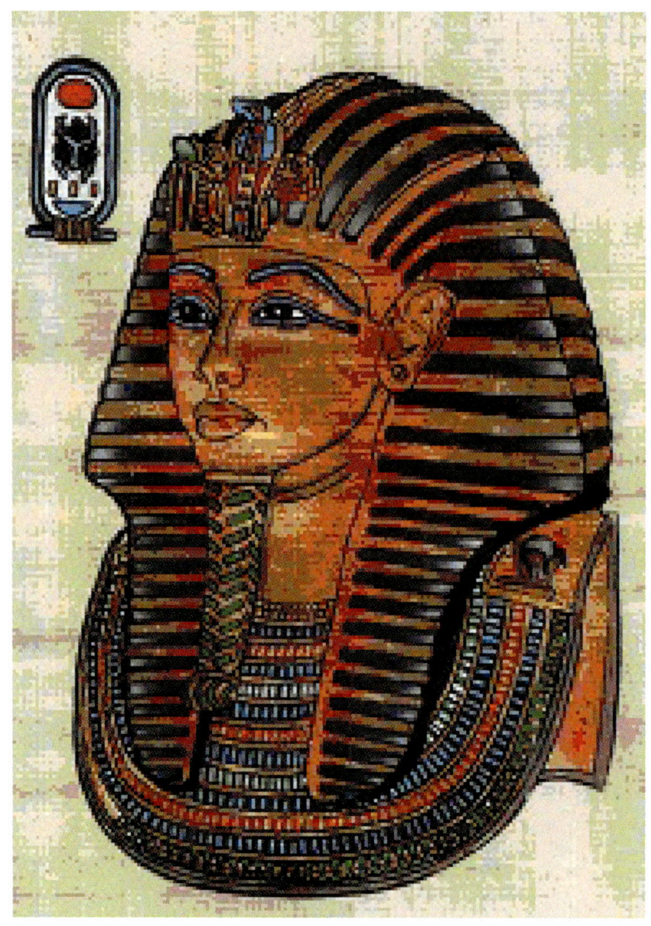

Coffin mask of Tutankhamun
(Note the cartouche insert to top left.)

If the Rosicrucian influence upon the life of Abraham Laverton is nebulous then that of the Freemasons is relatively clear if at times ambiguous. Equally the Freemason influence in the structure and content of the Window is loud and very visual. Examples of this can be seen in the border patterns throughout the design of the Window, the vine patterns incorporated into the middle two columns of the Window and the use of the font in the lettering of the legends (mottoes) in three of the Header sections.

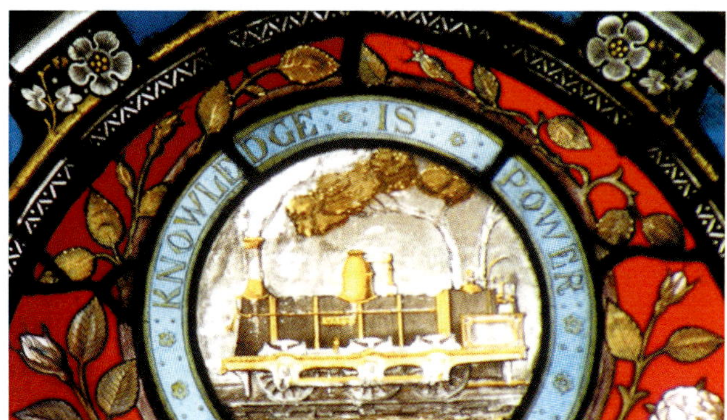

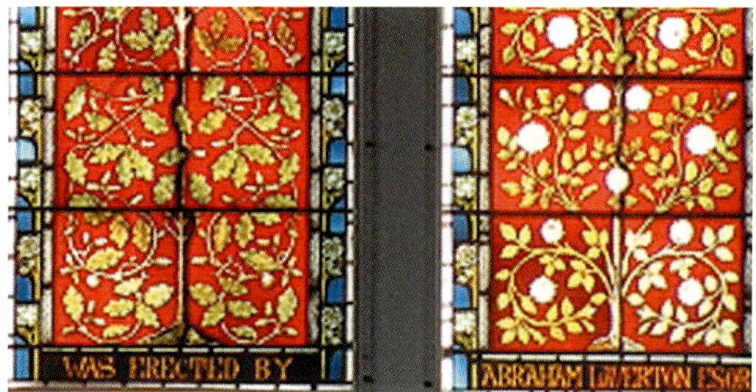

Traditional Freemasons' border pattern and font (above) and decorative vine pattern (below).

For anyone unsure who the Freemasons are, not least myself, by repute they constitute an international fraternity (brotherhood) based on 'love, faith and charity'. Their organisation is structured upon elaborate rituals, secret signs, passwords and the infamous handshake, much of which stems from Old Testament anecdotes and mythology.

The fashion to be an 'accepted mason' was in vogue in the 17th Century but the social and convivial fraternities that were spawned continue to the present day. The Masonic Order is forbidden to Roman Catholics but the impression today is of an organisation that few might object to even though it is essentially self-seeking.

In Westbury the White Horse lodge was founded in 1887 about a year after Abraham Laverton died. It continues with a small but sincere membership that reflects much of what the design of the Window was all about. The anti-slavery theme is a powerful undercurrent in Laverton's riptide of indignation at man's inhumanity to man. A much quoted passage that was fashioned at the time by the Freemasons and read as part of an appraisal of a paper on Morals and Dogma of the Ancient and Accepted Scottish

Rite of Freemasonry (prepared for the Supreme Council of the Thirty Third Degree for the Southern Jurisdiction of the United States: Charleston, 1871) stated:

Slavery is a disease whose shadow lies always upon America's threshold originating in the avarice and cruelty of the slave trade. I know it is an evil. Commercial greed values the life of men no more than it values the lives of ants.

So it is apparent that by this example Abraham Laverton's Rosicrucianism fitted hand in glove with the higher principles of Freemasonry but in the shape of an iron fist that struck out symbolically at the bad sides of his celebrated achievers in the Window and in particular Landseer.

It is more difficult to see where the Knights Templar fit into the big picture with any accord. Good medieval Christians as they were they slaughtered and went to their slaughter in their tens of thousands for century after century. Accumulated wealth was transient and ultimately no consolation for being burned at the stake. Yet, though their demise was categorical the likes of Isaac Newton persisted in exploring the heritage or the Poor Knights of Christ and of the Temple of Solomon even when he risked his own life. Little substantive evidence has been passed down to suggest that some love was lacking or overdone. The Templars had paid dearly for their striving towards some degree of autonomy and their reacceptance did not come easy.

The Templars set up local bodies and cultivated more distant ones but interest in them waned with time and in spite of the Window being a vehicle for radical re-ordering of ambitions no change ensued. The Knights Templar had long had their day and there was no reason to suggest a pending change in fortune certainly not by dint of the Priory of Sion that scholars universally accept was an out and out hoax that has engendered only scepticism.

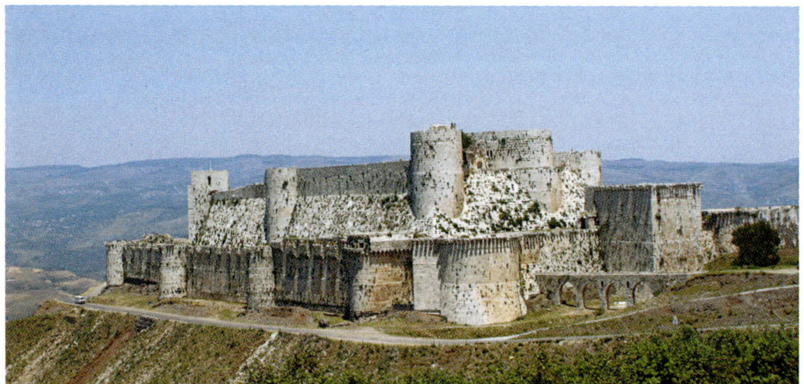

The fortress of Krak des Chevaliers (above) in modern day Syria was a superb Templar defensive structure. The present-day Templars and by association the Freemasons have no claim to any link with the Crusaders or the relict landscape features they left behind them, still less do the Rosicrucians or their breakaway groups like Militia Crucifera Evangelica or The Brothers of the Golden Cross. Such groups are modernist factions who regard Jesus Christ as an 'ascended master' and have less regard for him than their alchemy and natural sciences. Unfortunately Abraham Laverton does appear to have been associated with such parties.

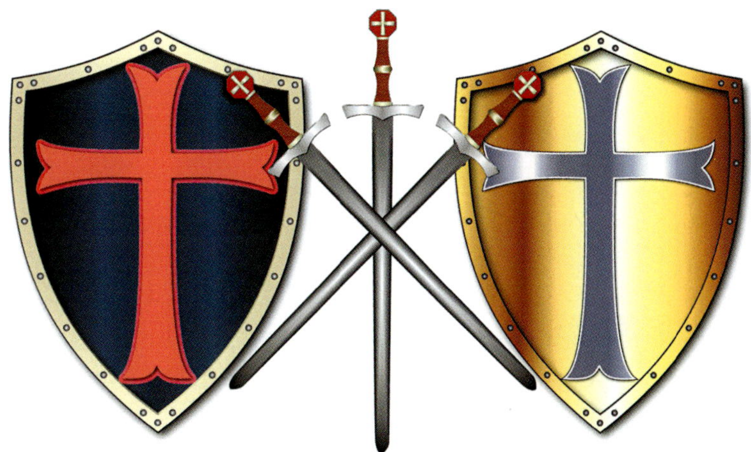

The example of the diocesan shield of Canterbury and of Salisbury that is illustrated earlier alongside the image of Abraham Laverton shares many characteristics with the typical shields of the Knights Templar shown above especially with regard to the configuration of the Maltese Crosses.

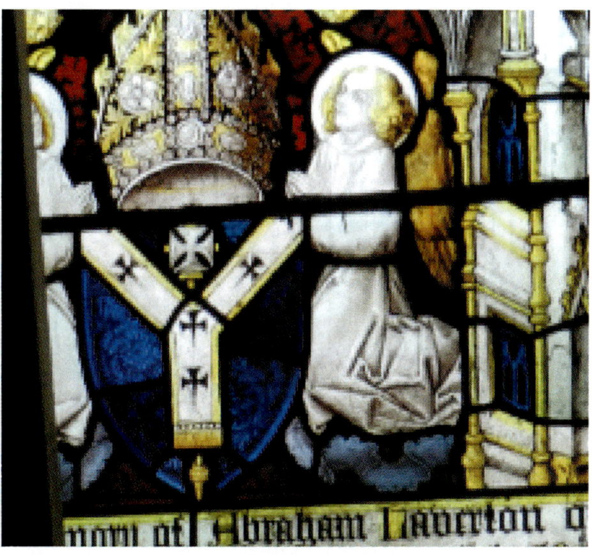

Shield of the diocese of Salisbury featuring in the stained glass tribute to Abraham Laverton in Westbury parish church.

Chapter 12
The 'Sciences' of Astrology and Alchemy

In the world in which we live today that sparkles with political corruption, religious hypocrisy, economic exploitation, social injustice, drug taking in sport, environmental abuse and misuse, double standards, back stabbing and back scratching by egomaniac, attention seeking, exploitative, power grabbing, self-promoting control freaks clothed in tieless grey suits or power-dressed in black, it is easy to be a cynic, wise to be a sceptic and compulsory to have a prenuptial agreement.

Was it ever any different? Originality is the rarest of gifts but if history tells us anything it is that life evolves in cycles that for the astrologer provide a recurring blank template. This enables the mystical structuring of lives that are defined by the terminology of the time and the vocabulary that most conveniently pigeon-holes figures of note.

'Group think' then takes over and in their contexts Pythagoras thought outside the box, Martin Luther challenged orthodoxy, Sir Roland Hill pushed the envelope (!), Icarus took a blue skies approach towards his mortality, Sir Clive Sinclair drove through change, Dr Dolittle executed a paradigm shift. Is it obvious where the sublime becomes the ridiculous?

The development of astrology and alchemy parallel each other quite clearly and are most absent from human record during times of war or serious conflict in a country.

In all our histories the fickle natures of astrology and alchemy have along the path of time been far worse. If you doubt it take that journey back along the Appian Way through the mass crucifixions of the first century BC, or journey into Stalingrad (now Volgograd) in the winter of 1942-43, or follow the tracks of the greatest of all deadly migrations, out of Africa, for now countless millennia.

Incredibly astrologists tell us amongst other things that according to our birthdates those who died in those hideous events (some of which persist timelessly) included individuals whose 'Fantasy Island love forecast' had 'Luscious Venus' revealing a former flame finding you 'in a sentimental mood'. Or for one in twelve of the 6,000 followers of Sparticus crucified to death their 'Stars' for August 72 BC may have read as follows if set 2,000 years or so later –

> This will go far to strengthen your personal centre of gravity so all aspects of your inner being can function more effectively and peacefully. Heart, body and mind aligned, this is your front line goal!

It seems beyond belief that intelligent men and women place any faith in such puerile drivel yet even in Abraham Laverton's day many of the educated classes called it science. Indeed, there are many societies today that regard astrology as conventional whilst others regard it as 'the lost science.'

That is not to suggest that in 1870s England astrology was in any way mainstream. It was by one devotee's description at best 'hiding in the corners' but like so many failed projects it learned the lesson that if you are backed up against an intellectual wall with nowhere to go then introduce a mathematical dimension for some academic 'street cred.' A nice long equation with some probability attached to the outcome usually goes down well and if that fails then introduce a constant.

The ultimate folly in employing that strategy was realised by a man named Albert Einstein. As Stephen Hawking points out in his book 'The Grand Design', in believing the Universe was static but finding his data did not fit the case he applied the cosmological constant to his equations of general relativity to represent a new antigravity force.

This turned out to be a blunder as the Universe has been shown to be expanding and Einstein to his credit subsequently acknowledged this.

What happened to bring Abraham Laverton's style of pseudo-scientific astrology out of its closet was a separation process from the misplaced association that had stalled it. This involved the codified restructuring of fundamental lines of key processes in alchemy and the parameters acting upon them. Astrological fortune made a u-turn in the early years of the 1900s and some degree of respectability has returned to it after hundreds of years of going down the academic tubes.

The misplaced associations still parasitically slide along in its wake but that aspect of astrology is a million miles away from the Indian cultures or the Japanese Shinto or Buddhist sects that have at least intellectually credible and theocratically tried and tested belief systems supporting them.

For many such groups astrological integrity is part of their culture, celebrations, politics and much more. For anyone who has ever slept outside in a desert, woken in the middle of the night and stared up at the canopy of stars there is a measure of wonderment that is beyond description.

There is little surprise that Abraham Laverton and his colleague William Jervis Stent were inspired to shape their masterpiece with its most extensive features being the asterisms from Pisces, Leo, Gemini and Taurus. On clear celestial nights over rural Wiltshire these would have been most familiar ceiling decoration and an inspiration for the proposed and most fantastic end to this book.

The place of alchemy in Abraham Laverton's life was, given that he was now surely a Rosicrucian, of some importance. 'Some' importance might be the beginning and the end of it and in the context of this book it almost was.

However it is to be noted in his quest to discover the Philosophers Stone Laverton knew that changing base metals into precious ones had a limited shelf life and eternal life could not last forever. That is to say, all the wealth in this world comes to nothing in the next world as whilst Heaven may await the Godly it does not mean that Judgement Day will be any particular man's salvation especially if reincarnation is around the corner.

However, temptation is an ugly word and the transmutation of lead into gold would have been fun to attempt. The fact of the matter is that for more than a century alchemy had also lost the kind of beneath the counter popularity that Isaac Newton would have got some anti-establishment thrill from. His defiance of the rule of law, state and canon in the emergent Parliamentary regimen of post- Commonwealth England was a measured indignant defiance of the Eucharistic Prayer respectively countenancing execution or eternal damnation. Those fears had passed into the mists of time for Abraham Laverton.

For the Victorians the search had become a quest for a better world. Spirituality was the touchstone for the new order and men like Robert Owen conceived of a Utopian socialist world being achieved through reform of the state, philanthropic benevolence and a pragmatic vision of what could be done to improve the working and living conditions of the masses. Enter from stage left Abraham Laverton.

Laverton had the alchemist's structured formula tattooed on the palimpsest of the Window in a layer of symbols that display clearly where he was coming from. Salt at Saltaire, Dale at New Lanark and Akroyd at Copley were contemporaries (or near contemporaries) who attempted to deliver improved living environments that would stimulate their populations to express a natural inclination to be responsible and caring, hard working and law-abiding, productive and more wealthy.

These were the aspirations of Abraham Laverton but he could not resist incorporating concepts such as the Rotation of the Elements that underpinned his own morality. It was thought to be the means of purifying the essence of a substance and raising it to its most sublime state as practised by alchemists. As well as having actuality Earth, Water, Air and Fire were for 2,500 years symbols of the elements that made up our world. Along with Spirituality great men like Empedocles and Aristotle stuck their necks out and tried to explain our material existence.

These men were for the best part wildly wrong but for the first recorded time men of science had something to build ideas upon regarding concepts such as fluidity and flexibility, expansion and contraction, psychology and personality, thought and intuition. For Laverton, the man who put the imp in palimpsest, there were many opportunities to play his games to mock and puzzle those with little depth to their thinking.

There is in his portfolio of cunning plans reference to the pelican, the pelican rampant, the pelican in her piety and in the context of Alchemy the two-bellied jar more correctly named the two-bellied reflux condenser or kerotakis, usually called a pelican.

Extraordinarily, the Rotation of Elements may be described by two laws of motion. These have no link to Kepler's ideas on planetary motion but do show Laverton's polymath versatility and are extraordinary because they apply to phenomena including species, nations, institutions and ideas. How many 'original' taxonomies have been extracted from that concept?

For the alchemist his case is a beaten docket. Once he refers to the 'spiral rotations' through the 'planetary spheres' he metaphorically falls backwards into the vagaries of Joachim Tanckius' early Seventeenth Century 'The Rotation of Elements by Master Rodianus.' It is one of many texts relating to alchemy that overworks the words 'secret' and 'mystical' but when it starts referring to the sex of elements it seems to have all the seriousness of W.C.Fields.

Abraham Laverton housed these ideas in his alchemical laboratory and copied them in part to the Window that already held symbols of Earth, Moon and Sun relating to eclipses. He contextualised the relevance of the properties of 'elements' by regarding them in part as the personalities of the four celebrated personages.

In the alchemical context the green and dark green rosettes represent the rotation of the four elements whilst the diagram following is a fascinating mathematical statement in fractal form pertaining to the structural form of the relationships that exist between the circles and spheres involved. Laverton must have understood this.

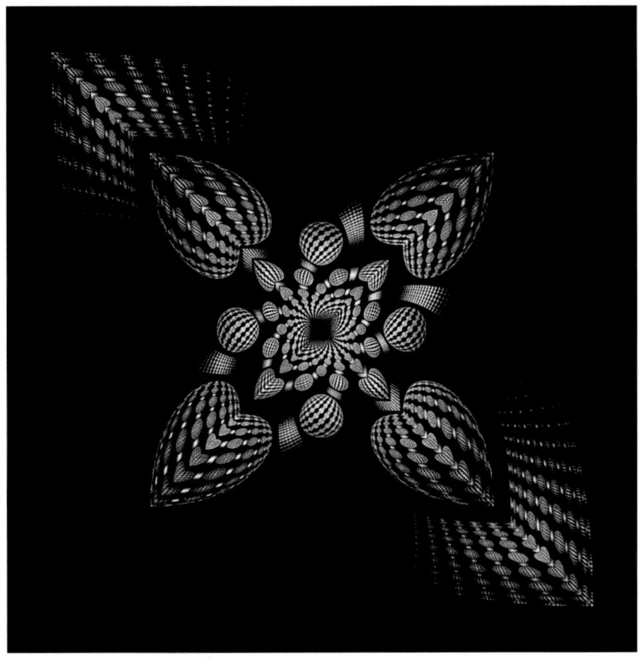

Left in fractal form is a representation of solar energy prominences that have usative effects in alchemy.

Broadly speaking Laverton's alchemy was dedicated to exploring scientific explanations of the world he lived in. As important to Laverton was the spirituality of alchemy and for him and many others transmutation was something they strived to achieve in the communities in which they lived.

Laverton built new housing, instituted a new educational and administrative centre and built a superb facility that was well ahead of its time. There is little in the town that he did not leave the mark of his commercial flair upon.

Without question the latter years of Abraham Laverton's life were spent in a quest to find the secret of everlasting life and what he could not concoct or engineer then, as we shall see, he imagined in the most spectacular way.

Chapter 13
World without end

With the wealth that Abraham Laverton left in his Will he could have made allowance for a much larger monument than he did to mark his burial place on his chosen plot in the Westbury cemetery. The cemetery is to be found adjacent to the Bratton Road some half a mile out of the town.

The cross that stands testimony to his memory is larger than most and is in the shape of a Celtic cross, as had been pointed out by a workman I consulted when searching for the Laverton plot. On first encounter I puzzled at this. The stone used on the monument is more expensive-looking than most but its resistance to the elements has over the years been weathered and reading the inscription is difficult.

Maybe by his own design he is slipping into anonymity as memory of him fades in the community. Did he foresee it happening this way?

Once I had got home that day some reading revealed that not all Celtic Crosses are Celtic crosses and the cross of the Rosicrucian movement is not a Celtic cross at all. in monumental form it takes a similar shape and this is what Abraham Laverton's cross may be identified as being.

Looking at his cross it is apparent was that he had made the most extraordinary contingency plan for remembrance that it is possible to imagine and for 140 years nobody has imagined it. Nobody has seen it. Nobody has understood the mosaic of clues, codes and ciphers pertaining to it and without that understanding and the knowledge associated with it nobody has had the inclination to do anything about it.

Yet it is the most brilliant and stunning way for anyone to conceive of immortalising themselves and deserves celebration if only for its audacious lack of modesty, its originality and its merits as a simulated trip into the cosmos.

The Laverton Experience as it may be called pulls together many of the aspects of this book and many of the creative thoughts of genius that Abraham Laverton gifted to the town of Westbury.

The first stage in this Experience requires the appreciation that Abraham Laverton's burial plot is (as near as could be) aligned along a east-north-easterly bearing extended from a line passing exactly through the centre of the long axis of the Function Room in the Laverton building.

Secondly, when the sun rises in midsummer over the horizon in a line with the gravestone cross above Laverton's plot it projects a shadowed cross (not unlike that used on a rifle sight) in the direction of the Laverton building. There is no direct visual line because of a rise in the land between the two points and the building of apartments as well as the planting of trees between the two reference points.

Within minutes the sun rises high enough to shine directly through the stained glass window and into the Function Room. What then occurs is that the images in the stained glass are projected onto the floor. Interestingly David Lawrence has seen a preservation order laying down conditions stating that the floor of that room must be especially cared for and polished to have the best possible shine and reflectivity. That is factor number three.

Fourthly as the condition of the Function room declines I have proposed that the Council organizes the laying of a quickly removable mirrored glass floor that would create the scenario for the 'piece de resistance'.

(Real mirrored glass floor panels are a small price to pay for the 'experience'.)

Ensuring enough people were present to make the operation go smoothly, at the moment of sunrise (approximately 4.30 a.m. on 21st June, Midsummer's day) as the sun shafts through the Window driving before it in that split second the shadowed cross of Abraham Laverton's monument the full stunning colour of the stained glass will flood the floor over and across the reflected ceiling.

For 140 years nobody seems to have realised the ceiling is painted darkest navy blue and covered in raised plaster-casted stars that will project through a mirrored floor to match the focal distance up to the ceiling and give the illusion to anybody stood at its elliptical centre of gravity of being suspended in space.

As the room lights anyone stood on the mirrored glass floor will encounter the spirit of Abraham Laverton as he intended stepping through the multi-dimensional portal of the Window to realise his goal of defying his own ephemerality.

It works, just as Laverton had planned fifteen years before he died. David Lawrence and I placed a single one foot square mirrored tile on the floor and stood back to see the effect of the ordinary reflection and it was stunningly impressive. David also found vivid descriptions of how the Function Room used to be lit by gas torches at night that produced superb lighting effects especially on the colours of the Window. Whether we could negotiate with the local Fire and Safety authorities to have unprotected propane lamps along one wall is maybe a step too far.

However this is what the man who associated his own mischievous spirit with imps and sprites was planning before the Laverton Institute Building was even built.

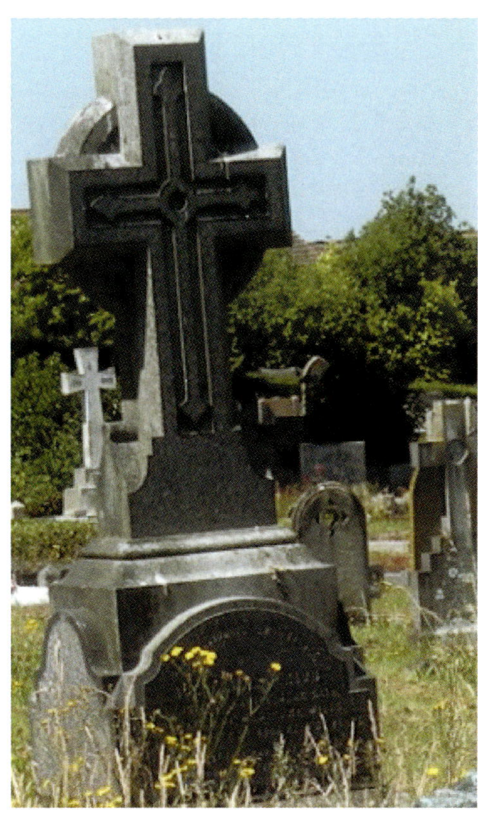

*The burial place of
Abraham Laverton
the headstone being a
Rosicrucian cross*

Sadly it will never happen like that in my lifetime. As noted the Window looks out onto a narrow pathway that is bounded to the east by an apartment block built around 25 years ago that shrouds the Window for most of the daylight hours. On the near horizon immediately beyond that twenty-foot trees further block any direct sunlight.

It is with such knowledge that it is possible for those interested in community heritage to move forward with the Window as a resource. Senior citizens groups, school parties, evening education classes, businesses and media organisations are obvious buyers into the Experience.

For Abraham Laverton the construction of the Laverton Institute Building and the incorporation of the stained glass Westbury Window was the culmination of a life's work. It is a summary of his understanding of the most significant influences upon his years as a Christian, a Rosicrucian, a Freemason and a Knight Templar and a statement of his advocacy for the recognition of honest endeavour over posturing and exploitation.

These things are manifest in his representations of injustices in the header images of the Window and the hidden better world that may be found if our viewpoints are simply turned on their heads. Equally he makes it clear that a privileged talent like Francis Bacon or a fragile genius like Richard Trevithick deserve fair recognition for their contributions to putting the Great in Britain.

He shows clear contempt for hollow attention seekers and egocentrics, even Isaac Newton, who would deny his fellow man any recognition for discovery or creativity if he could steal it first for himself.

Laverton places the heads of the personages in the Window deliberately as obstructions to light, life and learning and in a symbolic gesture makes the phenomenon of the eclipse an allegory for the just denial of those who would drown in glory whilst their fellow man choked on crumbs of comfort that fell from his banqueting table (to parody Ralph Waldo Emerson).

This book pays too little attention to the greater astronomical issues that Laverton incorporates in the Window and there is a case for a second volume that might deal with the mathematics alone. There is much yet to be revealed about the representations of planetary motion and the twin foci of ellipses, the orbital characteristics of the Earth's Moon, recurring measures of numbers to given powers as vectors, the significance of the cosmological constant, the frequency of portals in time and space as well as more difficult concepts such as those pertaining to how we measure time and cyclical events in our solar system and even general relativity.

The bottom line in the key humanitarian issues for Abraham Laverton is the respect that one man sustains for another. We see the case for the damnation of Shakespeare but Laverton places his case for such ostracising just below his favourite sprites and his own personal court of arms. Maybe this suggests a degree of contrition on Laverton's part and the Window operates as more of a restorative feature and salvation of Shakespeare's reputation than might have been thought when first noting his place in it?

When Laverton first designed the Window in the 1860s there was a veritable bandwagon riding slipshod over the reputation of the Bard. By the 1880s this tidal movement had quelled and more rational consideration was being given to the question of the authorship. It is even possible that the unfinished areas around the coat of arms are actually corrections in progress.

Whatever the case Shakespeare rode the storm and emerged in the Twentieth Century a more commanding iconic figure than at anytime since his death in the year 1616. The symbolic image of the goat has nevertheless to be tackled and resolved.

The extraordinary connections that Laverton would have had with his mentors in the organisations of the Brotherhood make for some special appreciation. Sources of materials for concocting the Philosophers stone were described in texts dating back to Zosimos of Panopolis in 300 BC/CE and Plato in his volume Timaeus. Laverton would have had some access to ancient texts including those from most respected Arabic sources such as Jabir Ibn Hayyan (Geber).

The combinations of basic and classical elements outlined by Geber would have been enough to have fixed the attention of Laverton as it had that of Isaac Newton two hundred years or so earlier. The aforementioned distributions of earth, fire, air and water have been found in manuscripts of Newton (that have survived) to contain strikingly comparable work to that of Gerber. Now, in the Window, there is clear evidence that Abraham Laverton was working towards the same end product, the Philosopher's Stone.

Interestingly, Laverton appears to parallel the orbits of the Moon with the elemental arrangement necessary for achieving the transmutation of metals no doubt using his beloved Pelican. To reiterate, he uses the same configuration to refer to the movements of the Moon in the alignment of the three objects that cause eclipses. It is conceivable he believed a common force was at work and if he did it was probably gravity.

I refer anyone doubting the credibility of such a multivariable analysis of the content of the Window to read David Chaim Smith's folio titled The Sacrificial Universe. In the form of triptychs and quadriptychs he offers folding plates that illustrate highly symbolic images drawn from books of hermetic mysticism that function on three levels; world, year and soul. There are striking comparisons to be made with the Westbury Window.

Appendix 1
Total Solar Eclipse of 1999

As an aside to the theme of Total Solar Eclipse noted in Chapter 10 it is coincidence to note that although I was living in Ireland at the time I spent the days around the E-Day of 10th August 1999 staying with a good friend in Westbury, Wiltshire.

I had long planned since the age of eight years that I would that I would witness the 1999 event that was featured and predicted in a set of encyclopaedias that my parents had bought my sister and me to help with our schooling.

For forty years I watched the calendar turn over never believing I would live to be so old. The year 1999 was as intangible as infinity at the age of eight but when it arrived and I rose at 4.30 a.m. to head on my motorcycle for Cornwall from Wiltshire it seemed the natural thing to be doing. On the A303 heading west it seemed half of England had the same destination and destiny.

Sometime around 8.30 a.m. I met up with another good friend in the town of Launceston who was also on his motorcycle out of Ireland. The weather forecast predicted cloud cover over much of Cornwall so following our instincts and the local radio weather forecasts we headed for the South Devon coastal town of Wembury that was being touted as likely to be clear as anywhere from cloud when the eclipse was due to arrive.

Wembury was, in spite of the dullness of the day, a coastal gem of a place. We managed to get some useful photographs although more by luck than judgement. Breaks in the thin blanket of cloud were brief and sporadic but of the 72 shots I fired off in the five or so minutes that the eclipse took to approach from the Atlantic, swallow little Wembury and pass by were reasonable. After some tweaking using the standard corrective software in more recent years they have with age improved like a fine wine. Not all have survived the duration but the half dozen or so included below are a meaningful record of the experience that will not be repeated in my lifetime

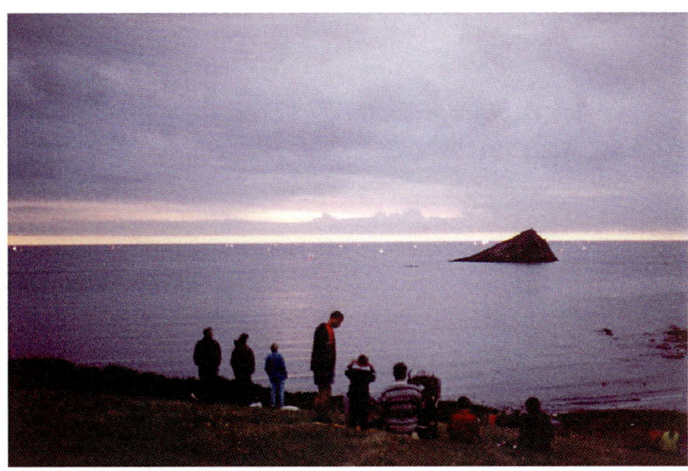

South Devon coast at Wembury as the wall of darkness sweeps from across the Atlantic

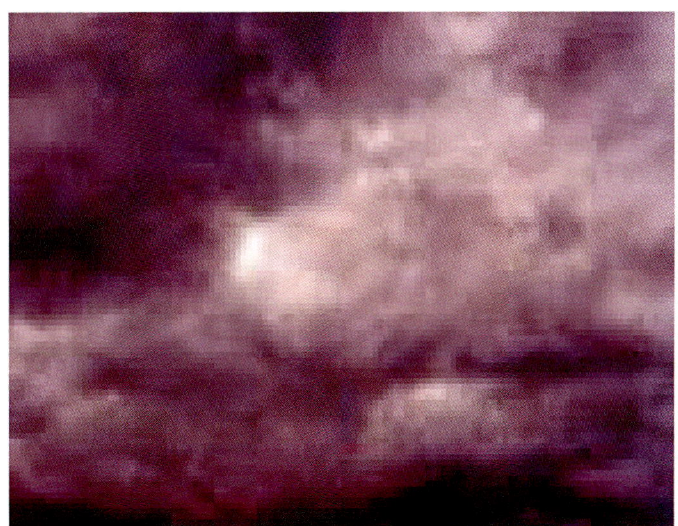

Disk of Sun visible left of centre of picture

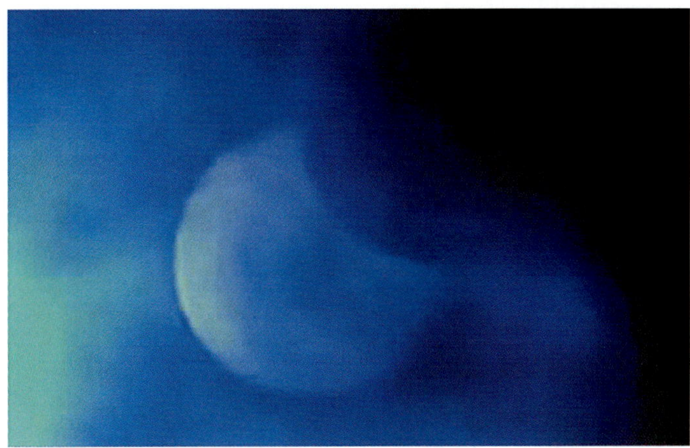

A gap in the cloud gave the last and best chance of a photo as focal plane shutter of camera then failed.

Appendix 2

This Appendix contains a sample outline for four columns and may be copied freely by the purchaser of this book.

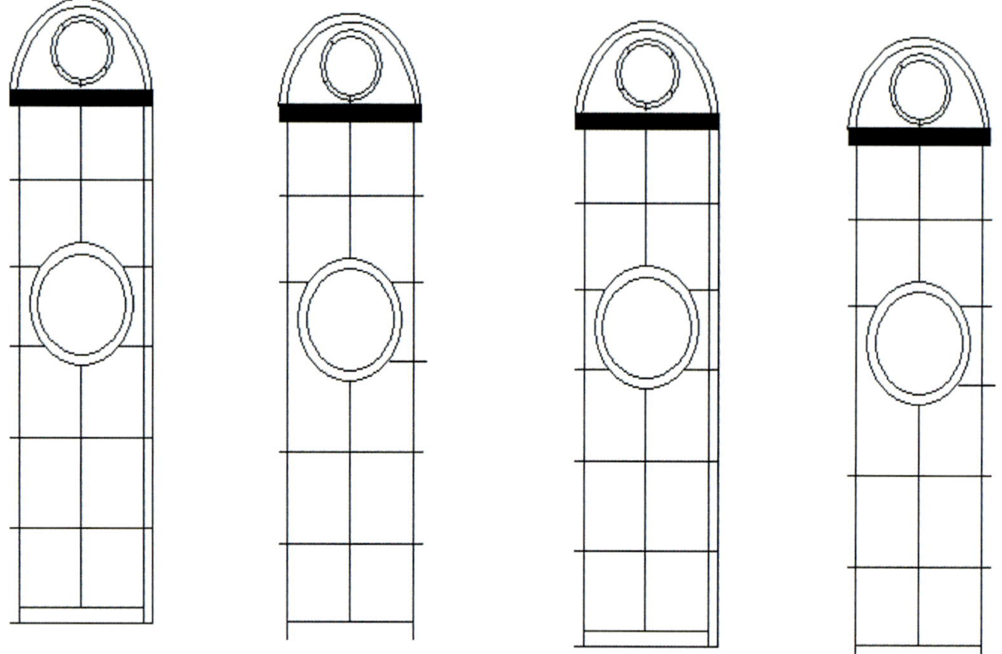

Sketch diagram for identifying the main panels in the Window

Sketch diagram for identifying main panels in stained glass units

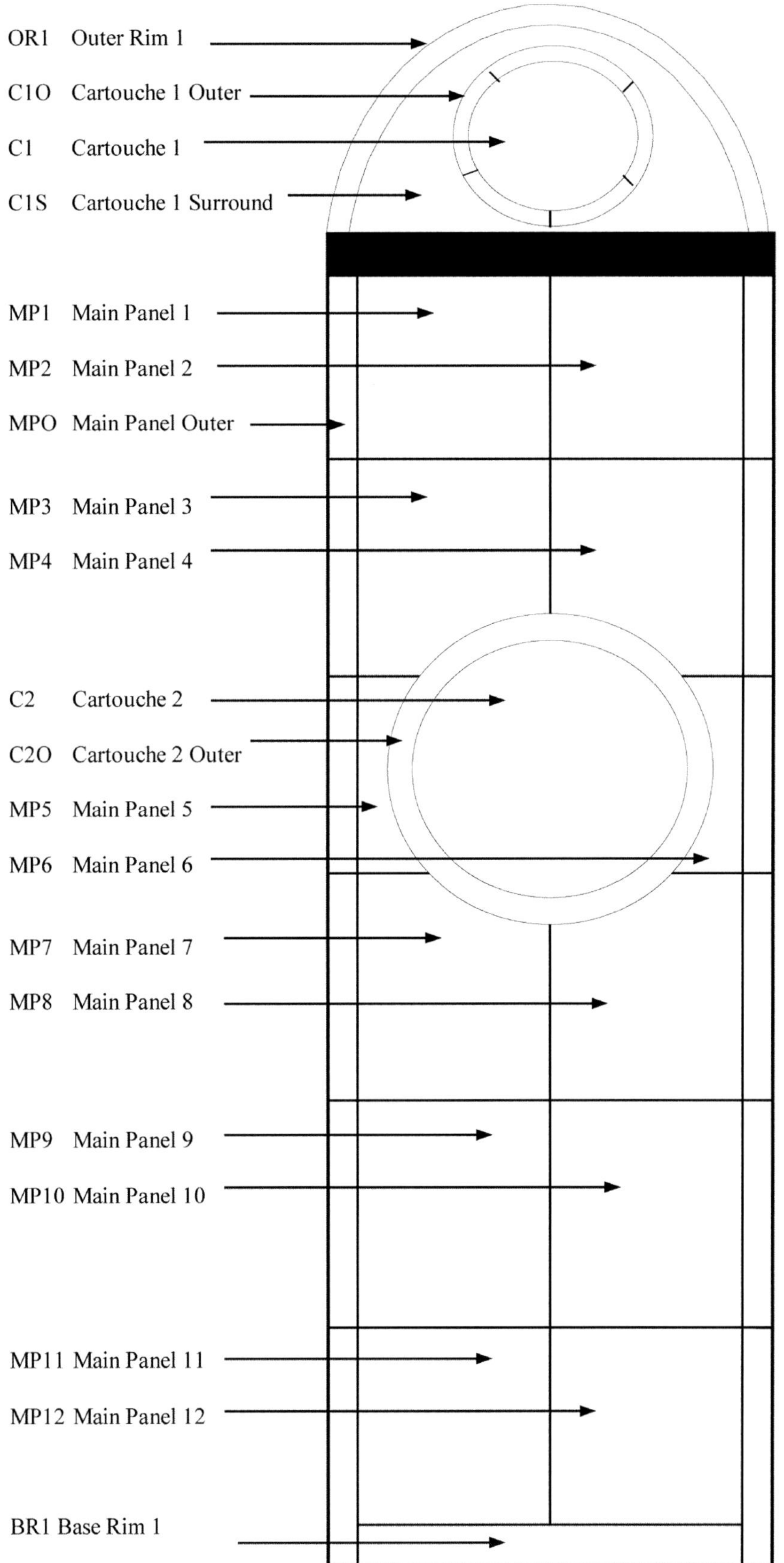

Figurative layout of the two centre columns

Appendix 3
Footnote on Slavery (Abraham Laverton's 'cause celebre')

It is difficult to rationalise how deeply the divide was in late nineteenth century Britain between those who abhorred slavery and those who saw it as a rightful inheritance that they should not have to forfeit no matter what laws were passed in their country or what moral indignation should be cast in their direction.

Much of the progress attained in giving rights of freedom to the masses in this country was rendered futile when their quality of life was taken into account. For many they had gained only the right to die on the street or work themselves to death at a coalface in their homeland or suffer even worse exploitation in a dominion of the Empire where every cloud had a silicosis lining.

Man's inhumanity to man in this context goes back to the dawn of time when the first hominids trod from the depths of Orduvai Gorge in Africa and called the land about them their homeland conceptualising the notion of ownership and the first property rights. Fast forward a few million years and dogs became property along with horses, livestock, crops and anything that had the notion of value attached to it, not least one's fellow man.

With the first civilisations on regional or national scales ownership became exploitation. With the first empires and warring factions exploitation became industrialised and feudal orders, caste systems and the like became parts of established hierarchies. The subjugation of one group by another for the purpose of control or gain operated candidly or subversively on local, regional, national or trans-national scales to the present day and will continue.

In the future those who look back to this period of history will reflect upon it at part of a time phase when technologies conjured up revolutionary tools of their trades such as the wheel, the printing press and computer chip. These will not be seen as successive times but parts of a whole and the generations that may number four per century will pass in as many blinks of the eye.

As we look back today upon the decline of the Roman Empire, the fall of Napoleon, passing meteors like Gustavus Adolphus, warriors such as Alexander the Great who died before his time or last in their lines such as Montazuma or Genghis Khan then we see the ends of phases of cruel exploitation of men by men. Slavery was a fundamental ingredient in successful empire building.

By Abraham Laverton's time empire building no longer needed to be by war or conquest. Industrial Revolution had broadened and accelerated the concept of economic imperialism. A new order of European nations emerged in the 1800s squabbling over ownership of Africa, the Americas and south east Asia in particular. Greed was their motivation and control freakery was manifest as their means to an end.

Laverton inherited his right to a share of the economic spin-offs from the decades of the Atlantic slave trade in particular but where contemporaries continued to nefariously exploit the cheap manpower of the African coastlands he focussed on a new world philosophy. Moral and religious outrage on a popular scale were the new weapons to counter the persistent abuses in the southern states of the USA in particular.

The moral high ground held by the Abolitionists was overwhelmingly supported by the British people but legal measures such as slave registration were still being introduced as late as 1854 as endorsements of the perceived success of emancipation. The trading legacy of the East India Company was not easily swept away. It was by the deeds of industrialists like Laverton with philanthropic leanings that the abolitionist zeal was made real and made to last and in the Westbury Window his indignation towards the undercurrent that supported the old order stood out, or at least it should have done. In the last two decades of his life Laverton witnessed the elimination of slavery across the Americas and as a Rosicrucian this would have been immensely satisfying.

However, Laverton still knew that the Americas were a small part of the problem and the demand for African slaves in the Islamic markets of the Near, Middle and Far East remained prolific. The tyranny of slavery persisted in the gulags of the satellite states of Stalinist Russia up until Nazi occupation when around twelve million labourers were moved from one hell to another when they must have thought things could not get any worse.

The shameful history of European slavery did not end in the 1880s as many might have us believe and Abraham Laverton's protestations in the Westbury Window have resonance up until very recent times if not today.

Appendix 4

The gate pattern of this wrought ironwork is found on the Internet community website 'Flickr'. It is the pattern found in columns 2, 3 and 4 of the Westbury Window but not column 1. Is this evidence if it is needed that Shakespeare was not as some have tried to argue a Freemason? Who knows? It is a pattern recurring in Freemasonry again and again.

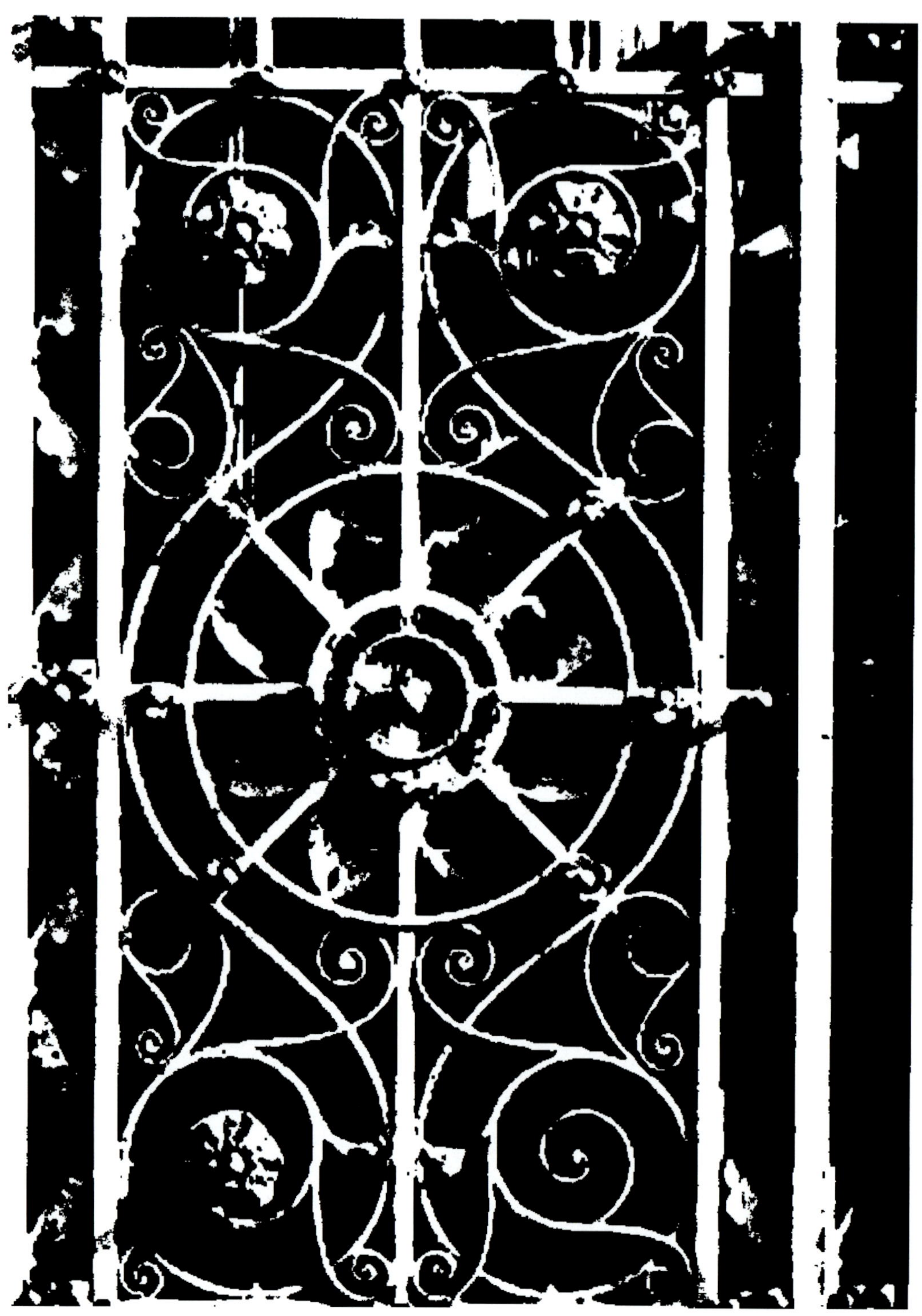

Appendix 5
Source and Reference Material

Pigpen cipher was a popular method of encrypting alphanumeric data and was used by the Freemasons for even the simplest of communications.   It goes by various names, there are varieties of it and similar codes exist from other interest groups. The standard form is shown below.

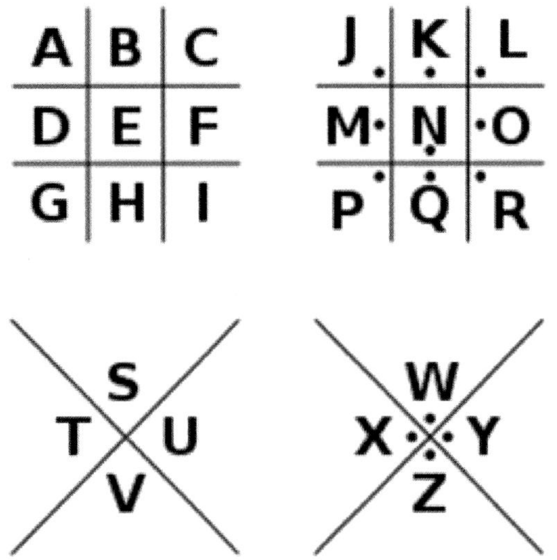

Can you work out the following message?

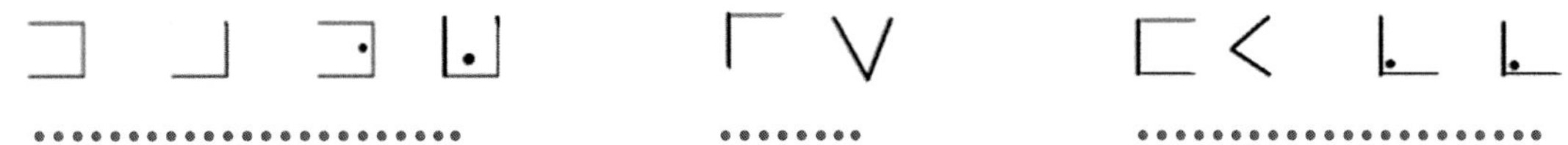

Photographs and Diagrams
(Databases of resources used)

There are approximately 100 images in the forms of photographs or diagrams used in this book. Some are used several times because of their importance to the investigation for which reason the actual number is 89 discrete images. Unless stated below the images in the forms of photographs and diagrams are all the property of John Powell. He either took and owns the photograph or constructed the diagram using a software package.

Exceptions include those listed below. Equivalent detail, or more, is archived for each image.

Royalty Free

Images licensed or Royalty Free
from 123RF

15	123RFQ	RF Purchase			WS		6222025 -11	
34a	123RFa	RF Purchase			WS&RFWS		26	23 - 24

Image acquired to provide comparison of William Shakespeare from the Window with work of an unknown portrait artist.

39	123RFb	RF Purchase			Bacon	8511638-32	69
46a	123RFY	"			Newton Cradle	14299825-40	68

Ref.www.123RF: Image credit: <a href='http://www.123rf.com/photo_11677816_nonthaburi-thailand--december-10-lunar-eclipse-over-thailand-sky-from-18-33-through-23-55-pm-on-dec-.html'>sailom / 123RF Stock Photo</a>
<a href='http://www.123rf.com/photo_18245008_an-image-of-a-nice-suneclipse.html'>markusgann / 123RF Stock Photo</a>

Images acquired to illustrate the phenomena of the total lunar and total solar eclipses.

68	123RFf	Photo			Orion	The Hunter 65	62
81	123RFx	Photo			DRing	-79	

Image credit: <a href='http://www.123rf.com/photo_4719222_orion-constellation-and-nebula.html'>peresanz / 123RF Stock Photo</a>
Asterism of Orion highlighting brightest stars and colours of stars etc. Used for illustration.

71	NASA	123RFf			Andromeda Spiral	67	64

Image credit: <a href='http://www.123rf.com/photo_15984414_andromeda.html'>iandoktor / 123RF Stock Photo</a>
Image credit: <a href='http://www.123rf.com/photo_15984414_andromeda.html'>iandoktor / 123RF Stock

Photo</a>   Used for illustration.

83a	123RFjh2	Portrait				Kepler	77	73

7	123RFz	Nikon P500			Pleiades	69	65
78	123RFs	Nikon P500			Ursa Major	69	65

jo

Image credit: <a href='http://www.123rf.com/photo_16575780_map-of-stars-focused-on-boreal-constellations-area.html'>procy / 123RF Stock Photo</a>

Image credit: <a href='http://www.123rf.com/photo_8285850_black-night-sky-with-the-constellation-of-great-bear.html'>goodday / 123RF Stock Photo</a>

Image credit: <a href='http://www.123rf.com/photo_8285850_black-night-sky-with-the-constellation-of-great-bear.html'>goodday / 123RF Stock Photo</a>

Image credit: <a href='http://www.123rf.com/photo_5235414_krak-des-chevaliers-citadel-tower-fortification-castle-walls--crusaders-fortress-syria.html'

<ahref='http://www.123rf.com/photo_16575780_map-of-stars-focused-on-boreal-constellations-area.html'>procy / 123RF Stock Photo</a>

90	123RFj	Krak Defence	5235414			Syrian fort	91
55	" "d	Big Dog	67075610	Ch7		51	
56	" " e	Traf Sq		Ch 7		52	
91	" k	Shields		Ch 12		92	

	Freeware 82	123RFg	Guttenburg	Hooper eliptical orbits	80

See website for conditions

Image credit: <a href='http://www.123rf.com/photo_5235414_krak-des-chevaliers-citadel-tower-fortification-castle-walls--crusaders-fortress-syria.html'
Image credit: <a href='http://www.123rf.com/photo_5235414_krak-des-chevaliers-citadel-tower-fortification-castle-walls--crusaders-fortress-syria.html'
Outstanding illustration of what The Templars used to be all about but have not been so for many hundreds of years.

Ref. 6222025 ml portrait derived from the Chandos engraving used for comparative study with that from the Window.

Image DataBase				
Page No.	Copyright	Camera	Description	Book Ref No
Cover Front	John Powell	NikonP500	Window	1
Inside Cover				
Cover Back	John Powell	NikonP500	ProsSqSunset	2
Inside Back	John Powell	NikonP500		
3	John Powell	NikonP500	Porchway	3
4	John Powell	NikonP500	WS	4
4	John Powell	NikonP500	IN	5
4	John Powell	NikonP500	JW	6
4	John Powell	NikonP500	EL	7
4	John Powell	Nikon P500	WTC Disclaimer	8
5	John Powell	NikonP500	Pelican 2nd&Dedication	9
6	John Powell	NikonP500	Frontispeace	
7	x		About the Author	
8	x		Foreword	
9	x		Foreword	
10	John Powell	Nikon P500	Foreword	10
11	x		Editor	
12	x		Acknowledgements	
13	x		Contents	
14	x			
15	123RFq	RF Purchase	White Horse	11
16	John Powell	Nikon P80	Function Room	12
17	x			
18	x			
19	x			
20	x			
21	John Powell	Diagram	PSqD	13
22a	John Powell	NikonP500	PSq1	14
22b	John Powell	NikonP500	PSq2	15
23	x			
24a	John Powell		Cemy Map	16
24b	John Powell		Mon Stone	17
25	John Powell	NikonP80	Plot	18
26	John Powell	DiagTWW	Column Plan	19
27	John Powell	DiagTWW	Single column	20
28	x			
29	x			
30				
31	John Powell	Nikon P80	WS	21
32a	John Powell	Nikon P80	WS2	22
32b	John Powell	Nikon P80	WS2 inverted	23
33	John Powell	Nikon P80	WS showing goat	24
34	John Powell	Nikon P80	WS3	25
34a	123RFa	RF Purchase	WS&RFWS	26
34b	John Powell	Nikon P80	WS&RFWSComparison	27
34c	John Powell	Sketch (JP)	WS&RFWSComp2	28
35	John Powell	Nikon P80	WS&Green Moons	29

36	John Powell	Nikon P80	Goat attack	30
37	x			
38	John Powell	NikonP500	Column 1 Header	31
39	123RFb	RF Purchase	Bacon image	32
40	John Powell		WScolSum	33
40a	John Powell	NikonP500	WS Zoom	34
41	John Powell	U/K	IN	35
42	x			
43	John Powell	U/K	Header 1	36
44	John Powell	Nikon P55	1st Col Headerdetail	37
45	John Powell	Nikon P80	Inverted	38
46	John Powell	Nikon P80	Andromeda	39
46a	123RFc	purchased	Ncradle	40
47	John Powell		JW	41
48	John Powell		Ursa Major column	42
48a	John Powell	Diag	Ursa Major column	43
49	John Powell	Diagram (JP)		44
49a	John Powell	Diagram (JP)		45
49b	John Powell	Diagram (JP)	Asterism Sketches	46
50	x			
51	x			
52	John Powell	Nikon P80	EHL	47
53	John Powell	Nikon P80	Grapes	48
54a	John Powell	Nikon	Inverted S	49
54b	John Powell	Nikon	Inverted L	50
55	123RFd	RF Purchase	St Bernard dog	51
56	123RFe	RF Purchase	Trafalgar Sq	52
57	John Powell	NikonP500	LionFace Trace	53
58	John Powell	NikonP500	Header Panel	54
58a	John Powell	NikonP500	Farleigh H	55
59	John Powell	NikonP500	Header Panel	56
60	John Powell	NikonP500	Mill Scenes	57
60a	John Powell	NikonP80	UpInv	58
61	John Powell	NikonP500	Mill Scenes	59
62	John Powell	NikonP500	Mill Scenes	60
62a	John Powell	NikonP500	Mill scenemore	61
63	John Powell	NikonP500	Loco Header	62
63a	John Powell	NikonP500	LocoWatt	63
64	John Powell	NikonP500	Strange features	64
64a	John Powell	NikonP500	Strange features2	65
65	John Powell	NikonP500	Seal Header	66
65a	John Powell	NikonP500	Laverton Institute	67
66	123RFff	NikonP500	Orion constellation	68
67	John Powell	NikonP500	Seale of town	69
68	David Lawrence	Canon	OrionA	70
69	JohnPowell	Canon	OrionB	71
71	123RFf	123RF	Andromeda Spiral	72
72	John Powell	Nikon P80	Ursa Major	73
73	123RFg	RF Purchase	Constellations	74
74	JohnPowell		Pleiades	75
75	x			

76	x			
77	John Powell	Nikon P500	Lunar Eclipse	76
78	123RFY	Nikon P500	Lunar Eclipse Transit	77
79	x			
80	John Powell	Diagram	Solar totec	78
81	123RFx	Photograph	Diamond Ring	79
82	123RFg	Guttenburg	Hooper eliptical orbits	80
83	123RFh	Diagram	Vine	81
83a	123RFh2		Kepler	82
83b	John Powell		Excerpt	83
84	x			
85	x			
86	x			
87	John Powell		North Transept	84
87a	Project Gutenburg	Cartouche		85
88	Street artist	Cartouche		86
88a	Street artist	Papyrus Sample		87
88b	Street artist	Papyrus Sample		88
89	Johm Powell	Nikon P80	Freemasons incidentals	89
89a			Laws of motion	90
90	123RFj		Krak	91
91	123RFk		Shields	92
91a	123RFkm		Diocese	93
92	x			
93	x			
94	x			
95	123RFp		Fractal	94
96	x			
97	x			
98	x			
99	John Powell	Nikon P80	Monument	95
100	x			
101	x			
102	x			
103	John Powell	Canon A1	Wembury 1999	96
103a	John Powell	Canon A1	Wembury 1999	97
103b	John Powell	Canon A1	Wembury 1999	98
104	John Powell	Diagram (JP)	Window Navigation	25
105	John Powell	Diagram (JP)	Window Navigation	26
106	x			
107	x			
108	Freeware	Diagrams	Vine3	99
109	Freeware	Diagrams	Pigpen	100
110	x			
111	x			
112	x			
113	x			
114	x			
115	x			

Bibliography

Abraham Laverton	Anthony Laverton	Silverwood
Alchemy, Science of the Cosmos	Burckardt & Stoddart	N/s (Not specified)
Cadbury Camelot	L. Alcock	T/H 1972
Elizabeth's Spy Master	Robert Hutchinson	W'feld & Nicholson
Exploring the Ancient World	Paul Bahn	AA
Greek Myths (2Vols.)	Robert Graves]	
How to Read a Church	David M. Rohl	Rider 2003
HMS Pinafore	W. Gilbert & A. Sullivan	Cramer
Incredible Visual Illusions	Al Seckel	Arcturus 2003
Knights Templar	Sean Martin	N.s
Knights Templar	Graeme Davis	N.s
Maisie and Me	Stella Ashton	Ex Libris
Man and His Symbols	Carl E Jung	Aldus Books 1984
Men & The Fields	Adrian Bell	Little Toller 1939
Night Sky	Kevin Tildsley	DK
RD Facts & Fallacies	(Team of Editors)	Readers Digest
Secrets of the Code	Dan Burnstein	Weiderfeld 2004
Stained Glass	Roger Rosewell	Shire Library 2012
The Ancient Burial		
Mounds of England	L. V. Grinsell	Methuen
The Atlas of Archaeology	M. Aston & T. Taylor	DK 1997
The Atlas of the Solar System	P. Moore & G. Hunt	Book Blub Assoc.
The Cathedral Builders	A.E.Brandenburg	Thames/Hudson
The Encyclopaedia of	Various	U/kn
The Sacrificial Universe	D.C. Smith	
The Times Newspaper Archive	Times News	Various
Wilts & Somerset Woollen Mills	Kenneth Rogers	Pasold Pub.
Wildlife		
World History		
The History of Wiltshire (1,1)	Eds. Pugh & Crittall	O.U.P.
The Illustrated Encyclopaedia		
of the Universe	Martin Rees	DK
The Pictorial Encyclopaedia	N/s	N/s
The Wiltshire Village Book	Michael Marsham	Countryside Books

The Secrets of Alchemy	Lawrence Principe	U/kn
Station X	Michael Smith Channel 4 Books	
The Story of Alchemy and . . .	M. M. Pattison	Muir 2012
The Test of Time	Richard Taylor	Rider 2003
The West Country	D. Parker	Batsford
Victorian Painting	Lionel Lambourne	Phaidon 1990
Wilts/Somerset Woollen Mills	Kenneth Rogers	Pasold Research
Wiltshire of 100 Years Sgo	David Buxton	Alan Sutton

Bibliography of website addresses

http://www.freemasonry.com/alchemy_freemasonry.html	21/05/2013
http://theabysmal.wordpress.com/tag/equinox/	21/05/2013
https://en.wikipedia.org/wiki/I_Ching	21/05/2013
http://www.thelaverton.co.uk/laverton-hreitage/history-development.html	21/05/2013
http://dummies.com/how-to/content/easy-masonic-ciphers-to-figure-out.html	24/05/2013
http://www.horizonenergycorp.com/hpo/constellations/bible.htm	24/05/2013
https://en.wikipedia.org/wiki/stained_glass	26/05/2013
http://suneartday.nasa.gov/2011/articles/ttt_72.php	03/06/2013
http://web.eecs.utk.edu/~mclennan/BA/RE.html	04/06/2013
http://en.wikipedia.org/major_chord	04/06/2013
https://www.asme.org/engineering-topics/articles/transprtation/richard-trevithick	07/06/2013
http://en.wikipedia.org/wiki/Ursa_Major	08/06/2013
http://hypertextbook.com/fgacts/2000/IlanaEpstein.shtml	08/06/2013
http://www.locationworks.com/sunrise/5070.html	08/06/2013
http://www.math.nus.edu.sg/aslaksen/gem-projects/hm/0102-1-stonehenge/sun.htm	09/06/2013
http://www.en.wkikpedia.org/wiki/Saros_(astronomy)	10/06/2013
http://eclipse.gsfc.nasa.gov/Sesaros/Sesaros.html	12/06/2013
http://calendars.wikia.com/wiki/TheAbysmal_Claendar	12/06/2013
http://www.edkohout.com/mundane/nyse.html	12/06/2013
http://en.wikipedia.org/wiki/William_Shakespeare	21/06/2013
http://www.newadvent.org/cathen/13193b.htm	21/06/2013
http://en.wikipedia.org/wiki/Rosicrucuanism	23/06/2013
http://en.wikipedia.org/wiki/Satanism	23/06/2013
http://en.wikipedia.org/wiki/Shakespeare_authorship_question	24/06/2013
http://en.wikipedia.org/wiki/Abraham_Laverton	01/07/2013
http://en.wikipedia.org/wiki/Wheel_of_the_year	01/07/2013
http://en.wikipedia.org/wiki/Rosy_Cross	03/07/2013
http://www.rosicrucian.org/about/mastery/mastery08history.html	03/07/2013
http://the-moon.wikispaces.com/Retro_Reflection+phenomena	07/07/2013
http://www.gutenberg.org/files/24667/24667-h/24667-h.htm	11/07/2013
http://www.youtube.com/watch?v=z_DDXnuzEB4	13/07/2013
http://www.nasa/audience/formedia/features/MP_Photo_Guidelines.html	15/07/2013
http://www.newadvent.org/cathen/13193b.htm	25/07/2013
http://eclipse.gsfc.nasa.gov/Sesaros/Seperiodicity.html	27/07/2013
http://en.wikipedia.org/wiki.Ad_orientem	02/08/2013
http://mysteryoftheiniquity.com/2012/11/10/north-the-hidden-one/	03/08/2013
http://www.sacred-texts.com/eso/sta/sta19.htm	03/08/2013
http://hyperphysics.phy-astr.gsu.edu/hbase/music/just.html	03/08/2013

http://www.rosicrucian.com/2qa/2qaeng06.htm   06/08/2013
http://en.wikipedia.org/wiki/Month   14/08/2013
http://www.timeanddate.com/worldclock/astronomy.thml?n=2477   16/08/2013
http://thelunarsaros.blogspot.co.uk/2009/05/case-study-using-lunar-saros.html 21/08/2013
http://www.cuttingedge.org/news/k1001.cfm   23/08/2013
http://www.nature.com/news/2011/10616/full/news.2011.372.html   28/08/2013
http://www.wildlifeartjournal.com.lblog/257/wild-man-the-brilliara
http://theabysmal.files.wordpress.com2008/11/ma_mandala.jpg
http://theabysmal.files.wordpress . . .
http://www.biblenews1.com/hands/handi.htm   27/09/2013

Postscript

As measures of how difficult it is to see what Abraham Laverton and his team of designers and artisans were intent on hiding in the Window there are included here three scaled up examples of images that I suggest are first looked at by the reader. In these photographs are details not imagined at the start of the book.

Unless such basic enhancement is facilitated viewers may never know what they are missing in terms of detail and quality. The casual passer-by misses much just as Laverton intended. The three images selected as examples are -

1 James Watt

2 The goat's head at the mausoleum in the Bratton Road Cemetery

3 The Great Seal of Westbury

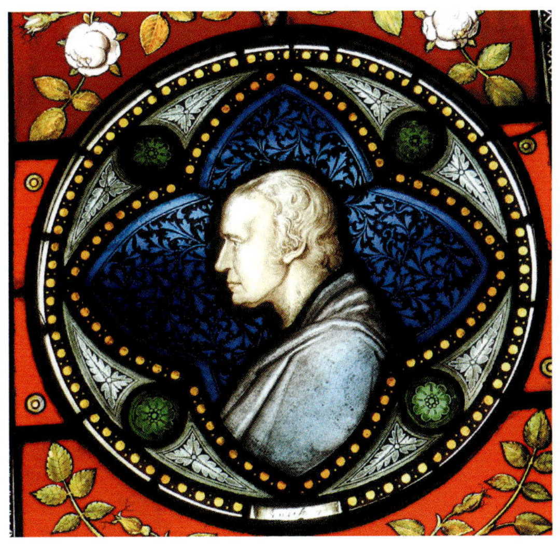

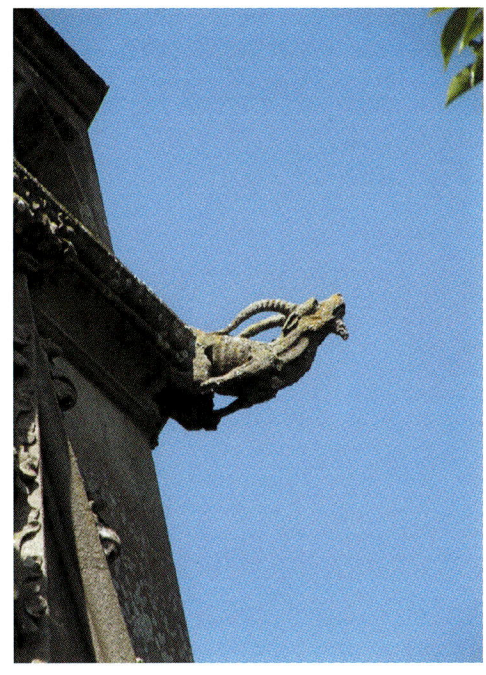

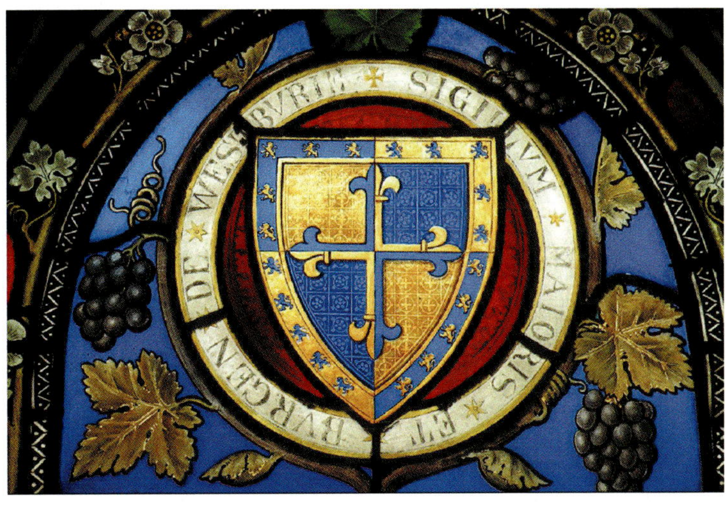